the kitchen garden

the kitchen garden

simple projects for
the weekend gardener

Richard Bird

photography by Jonathan Buckley

RYLAND
PETERS
& SMALL

LONDON NEW YORK

For this edition:

Designer *Sonya Nathoo*

Senior editor *Clare Double*

Production *Sheila Smith*

Art director *Gabriella Le Grazie*

Publishing director *Alison Starling*

Illustrations *Richard Bonson*

First published in the United Kingdom in 2000
and reissued with amendments in 2005
by Ryland Peters & Small
20–21 Jockey's Fields
London WC1R 4BW
www.rylandpeters.com

10 9 8 7 6 5 4 3 2 1

ISBN 1 84172 803 9

A CIP record for this book is available from the
British Library.

Printed and bound in China.

contents

introduction

kitchen gardening combines the production of fresh vegetables and fruit for the kitchen with the aesthetics of the ornamental garden; it is tasty and pretty, making it one of the most satisfying forms of gardening.

There is nothing like the taste of fresh fruit and vegetables. The fact that you pick or harvest your own produce just minutes before it appears on the table means that your food has a flavour and freshness that you will never get from a grocer. Until you have grown your own, you have missed a culinary experience that will top all others.

Vegetables are decorative plants in their own right, and many of the props used in vegetable gardening, such rhubarb forcers, add to their visual impact. Some vegetable gardens are created specifically for their attractive qualities, but even those laid out along more traditional lines will give a great deal of pleasure. There is no need for a huge space when planning a vegetable garden: big areas undoubtedly have the advantage of large-scale production, but enough can be harvested from the smallest gardens to make the effort worthwhile.

This book sets out a series of projects that contain both inspirational and practical ideas for gardens of all sizes – from a roof garden to a large plot. Even a patio without any visible soil can be turned into a productive area.

Richard Bird

vegetable, fruit and herb plots

A vegetable garden, or potager, is more than just a means of growing vegetables. It can be very decorative in itself, and is often the ideal solution in a garden where space is at a premium. A plot can be anything from a simple rectangle with rows of vegetables to a more complex potager, in which every plant is carefully positioned to create a satisfying and balanced picture. The garden can be broken down into various areas, each with its own purpose or decorative quality. Herbs can be grown in a knot garden, for example, or strawberries can be grown within rectangles of low box hedging. The possibilities are endless.

above left Mixing flowering plants with vegetables adds another dimension to the potager. Here lavender bushes line a beetroot bed.

below left Fruit trees add vertical interest to a kitchen garden as well as forming part of the permanent structure. They also, of course, give fruit.

above Cages that provide protection from birds should not be used just for fruit; many vegetables also need guarding. Here an attractive mixture of vegetables, fruit and vulnerable flowers is grown in a home-made cage.

right Large flower pots, old-
fashioned cloches, rhubarb
forcers and even scarecrows can
be used to break up expanses
of vegetation in the garden.
Here a row of terracotta pots
nestles among endive.

right Even very common
vegetables have varieties of
ornamental value. Lettuces,
for example, are available in a
range of reds and red-browns,
and with differently shaped
leaves, including feathered
and frilly forms.

below This potager features
a strong symmetrical design,
prominent ornaments and
vegetables and herbs that
are allowed to flower.

potager

A well-maintained vegetable garden is decorative in its own right; however,
it is possible to go one step further and produce a kitchen garden that is not only
productive but also designed to look attractive. There are many ways to do this, but
basically it is a question of combining the colours, shapes and textures of plants in
a well-considered layout. Paths, beds and ornamental structures can all play valuable
roles. Such a garden may be a single bed or a combination of several.

MATERIALS & EQUIPMENT

terracotta pots • gravel • edging bricks

spade • fork • rake • trowel • pegs and string

bottle and light-coloured sand

measuring stick • watering can

garden roller

vegetable seed and plants in variety

plenty of well-rotted organic material

1 planning
Draw up a plan of your desired potager. In the first instance it should include only the bare bones and permanent features of the vegetable garden, including paths, edging and any hedges and trees.

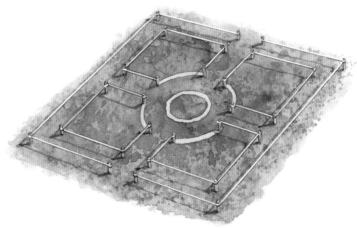

2 marking out the plot
Thoroughly prepare the plot by removing all weeds and moving existing plants that are in the wrong place. Transfer your drawn plans to the ground using pegs and string. Curved lines may be laid out using lengths of flexible hose. Double-check all measurements – they must be right first time.

3 laying the edging and path
It is not essential to fix the paths permanently in concrete; indeed you may wish to enlarge or redesign the potager after a few years. To keep your options open, simply firm down the soil in the path areas with a garden roller and roll in several layers of gravel. Alternatively, lay paving slabs on a bed of sand. If using gravel, put the brick edging in place before laying the path.

4 planting
Dig the bed areas, adding as much organic material as possible. Draw out the planting plan on each bed using a bottle of sand as an oversized pencil. Sow the seed or set out the plants according to your needs. Planting a box hedge around the potager will give it a distinct boundary. Set out the young box plants at 15 cm (6 in) intervals (see page 24).

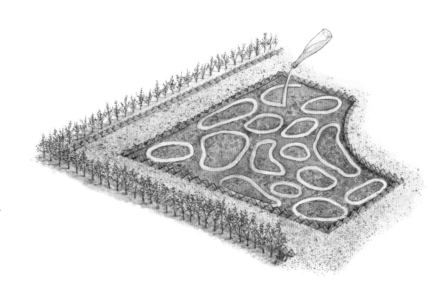

5   mature vegetable plot

Try to keep the potager looking its best throughout the summer. Harvesting plants leaves gaps that can upset the design, so keep a few young plants growing on in pots and trays to plant out as replacements. Quick-germinating, fast-growing crops, such as radishes, which can be sown *in situ*, can also be used as fillers.

filling gaps in the design
Terracotta pots can be planted up and placed either as a
permanent part of the display or to fill a gap temporarily.
Keep several pots in reserve to use whenever there is a blank
space or to replace a pot that has finished.

13

traditional vegetable bed

The traditional vegetable plot is usually arranged in rows. It is set out for practical rather than aesthetic reasons but, carefully planned, it can be visually attractive as well as productive. The sheer variety of leaf forms and colours, as well as variation in height and breadth, creates a decorative pattern that is difficult to better. Gaps between the rows allow for easy access to the vegetables, both for cultivation and for harvesting.

MATERIALS & EQUIPMENT

spade • fork • rake

draw hoe • pegs and string

vegetable seed and plants in variety

well-rotted organic material

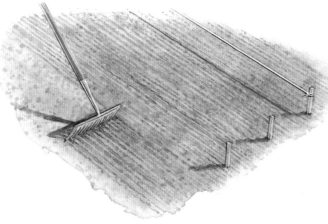

1 preparing the ground

Prepare the soil thoroughly in the autumn, digging in plenty of well-rotted manure or compost. In spring, rake the soil surface to give a fine tilth. Use a garden line or string and pegs to mark out rows for planting, ensuring that there will be sufficient space between the rows when the plants are mature.

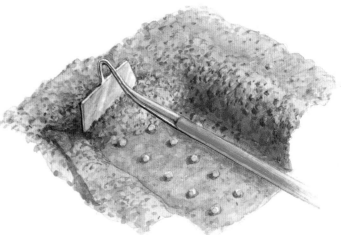

2 sowing

Most seeds can be sown directly outdoors; follow the guidelines on the packet. Some can be broadcast onto raked soil, then lightly covered over; others should be sown into a narrow drill (see page 20). Plants that are grown close together, such as peas, should be sown two abreast in a wider drill, about 25 cm (10 in) across, made using a draw hoe.

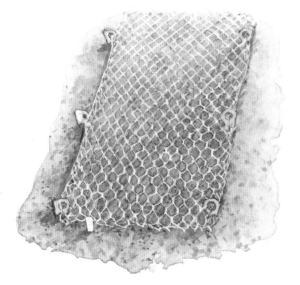

3 protecting the seeds

After sowing in a drill, cover with netting to protect the seeds from birds. Covering the soil with an organic or plastic mulch helps retain water and chokes out weeds, greatly reducing the time needed for cultivation. Organic mulch, such as grass cuttings, should be applied between the rows once the seedlings have become large enough not to be smothered.

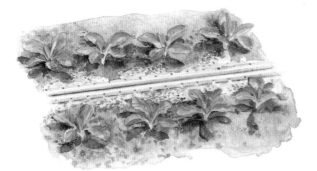

4 watering

All vegetable seeds and seedlings should be kept well watered; many, including the brassicas and lettuces, need intensive watering for a good crop. Using a seep hose laid between the rows cuts down on labour; the hose can be moved easily across the whole vegetable patch.

5 extending the growing season

The season for vegetables such as spinach, peas and brassicas can be extended well into autumn and early spring by growing them under cloches. For example, spring cabbage planted under cover in October will be ready in February. Lightweight, plastic cloches are available, but it is worth seeking out glass ones that enhance the character of the garden.

6 care and maintenance

A low box hedge around the bed improves the garden's appearance but has no other practical value. A taller hedge or fence is needed if shelter from winds is the goal. The vegetable bed should be kept well watered and regularly weeded. Crops grown under a cloche require extra watering; and any plants started off under cover should be hardened off before exposure to the elements, otherwise their growth may be stunted.

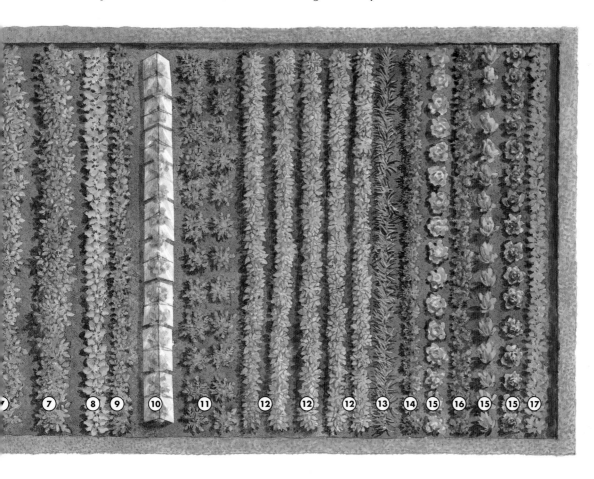

plant list
1 cabbages
2 Brussels sprouts
3 tomatoes
4 leeks
5 onions
6 peas
(on pea sticks)
7 potatoes
8 kohlrabi
9 turnips
10 spring
cabbages
11 celeriac
12 French beans
13 shallots
14 flat-leaved
parsley
15 lettuce
16 parsnips
17 beetroot

salad bed

All vegetables are best appreciated when fresh, and salad plants in particular
are crispest and fullest of flavour immediately after picking. Growing your own lets
you harvest as much or as little as you want, and allows you to combine, in a single
salad, the flavours of a wide variety of lettuces. If bought from the shop or market,
this culinary effect would be prohibitively expensive; added to this is the great
satisfaction of growing your own vegetables.

MATERIALS & EQUIPMENT

spade • fork • rake • hoe

garden line or pegs and string

trowel

seed of salad vegetables in variety

well-rotted organic material

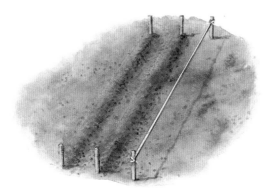

1 marking out the plot

Prepare the soil by digging thoroughly and working in plenty of organic material. Using a garden line, mark out the rows allowing for the size of the full-grown plant plus 30 cm (12 in) between each row for easy access. If you do not have a ready-made garden line, pegs and string can be used in the same way.

2 planting

Using the edge of a hoe, make a shallow channel, or drill, along the lines marked out. Scatter seed evenly along the drill, cover with soil and firm down gently before watering. In very wet conditions, line the drill with dry sand before sowing; in dry conditions water the drill before sowing and lightly press the seeds down into the soil.

3 thinning and watering

Even when sown sparingly, most salad crops will need thinning out. When the seedlings are big enough to handle, pull out surplus plants, leaving single plants at the required intervals (equivalent to the width of a mature plant). Most salad crops do best if they are kept growing – any check in growth will affect size and taste – so keep the plants well-watered in dry weather. The best method is to water each row individually with a watering can, making certain that the soil is thoroughly soaked.

4 salad throughout the year

Salad crops are needed year-round; but if lettuces, for example, are sown all at once then they will crop together and be over in two weeks or so. Rather than sowing full rows, it is better to sow part of a row every two weeks. Many loose-leaf 'salad bowl' lettuce varieties resprout to give a second or even third crop when cut at the base. Such cut-and-come-again varieties are an excellent way of making use of limited space.

5 sowing radishes

Harvesting salad crops inevitably leaves ugly gaps in the rows. To make the best use of space these can be filled by sowing radish seed; radishes are quick to mature and are ready for the kitchen just 3–4 weeks after sowing.

6 pest control

Perhaps the most destructive salad crop pests are slugs, and you must reduce their numbers or there will be little left for you to eat. An effective way to kill them is to set a beer trap – a jar, partly filled with beer, set into the soil. Alternatively, simply remove the slugs from the plants at night, when they are most active.

planting celery
Dig plenty of manure into the soil – celery demands high levels of nitrogen. Raise young celery plants from seed in the greenhouse. In spring, set these small plants out in a narrow trench.

7 maintenance and harvesting

Hoe along the rows and round each plant to remove weeds. Leaf vegetables cannot be stored; cooked puréed tomatoes can be frozen; celery can be left in the ground until needed.

blanching celery
When the celery reaches a height of about 30 cm (12 in), wrap corrugated cardboard round the stems, leaving the leaves free. Fill the trench with earth, drawing it up around the cardboard 'sleeve'.

plant list
1 spring onions
2 beetroot
3 radicchio
4 cos lettuce
5 salad bowl lettuce
6 radish
7 ridge cucumbers
8 celery
9 tomatoes
(staked not bush)

strawberry bed

Although strawberries are widely available from shops all year round,
nothing tastes quite like those eaten straight from the plant. Strawberry plants are
relatively cheap, easy to grow and look attractive whether in a bed or grown together
in a container. With careful selection of varieties, they can be harvested from late
spring right through to the autumn. The fruit is suitable for eating as it is,
preparing for meals or drinks, or turning into preserves.

MATERIALS & EQUIPMENT

posts, flower pots and netting

straw for mulching

spade • fork • trowel • rake

garden line or pegs and string

measuring stick • hedge clippers • watering can

7 *Buxus sempervirens* 'Suffruticosa' per metre (3 ft) of hedging

5 strawberry plants per 2 metres (6 ft) of strawberry row

2–3 buckets of organic matter per square metre (yard)

1 preparing the bed

Mark out a plot using pegs and string, checking that the corners are right angles. An area of about 4.5 x 3 m (15 x 10 ft) will provide a generous crop.

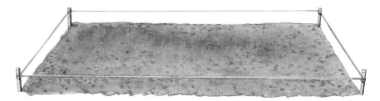

2 planting the bed surround

Strawberry beds look attractive if they are surrounded by low hedges or raised boards. Plant young box, preferably a dwarf variety such as *Buxus sempervirens* 'Suffruticosa', in the spring at 15 cm (6 in) intervals around the bed. Pinch out the tips so that the plants bush out, which may take several years. Keep the box clipped back to the height and width required.

3 planting the beds

Prepare the ground thoroughly by removing all weeds and digging in plenty of well-rotted organic material. In late summer, buy plants that are guaranteed free from disease. Plant these at 40 cm (16 in) intervals in rows that are 60 cm (2 ft) apart. Water thoroughly; keep watered until they are established.

4 mulching

In the late spring, just as the fruit is beginning to swell, mulch underneath the plants with straw, tucking it up under their leaves and stems. This helps keep the fruit off the ground. Alternatively, black polythene can be placed under each plant.

board surround
A *board surround* to the strawberry bed not only looks good but is easier to prepare than a box hedge border. The bed can be built up by filling in with plenty of well-rotted compost and good quality loam, creating a fertile growing medium for the strawberries. The board edges also help to prevent straw in the bed from being blown or scattered.

pole fence surround
An alternative to a board surround is to use hazel or chestnut poles. These should be 2.5 cm (1 in) in diameter and split in half lengthways, then nailed to uprights that have been driven into the ground, or woven between them. Low woven hurdles can also be bought as ready-made panels.

5   protecting your crop
Ripening fruits are a target for birds in late spring. To protect your strawberries, place short posts in the ground and drape netting over upturned flower pots – these allow the net to be moved without damaging the mesh. Weight the netting at the base.

6   mature beds
Pick the strawberries by pinching through the stalk to avoid bruising the fruit. When growing strawberries, two beds should ideally be prepared because the plants begin to deteriorate if grown for more than three years in the same place. Use the beds alternately for strawberries.

taste of the orient

Traditionally, vegetable gardeners are a very conservative species, adopting new plants rather slowly. For example, both potatoes and tomatoes took several centuries before they were widely grown in Europe. But in recent times gardeners have become more adventurous, matching the exciting developments in the kitchen and restaurant by growing more and more exotic and oriental vegetables.

MATERIALS & EQUIPMENT

bricks • cement • concrete

10 x 5 cm (4 x 2 in) wood for frame

2.5 x 2.5 cm (1 x 1 in) wood for runners

5 x 5 cm (2 x 2 in) wood for frames of lights

galvanized screws • glass cut to size

glazing sprigs and putty • wood preservative or paint

spade • bricklayer's trowel and line • spirit level

saw and rebate saw or plane • hammer • screwdriver

ruler and pencil • fork and rake • pegs and string

seed and plants in variety

well-rotted organic material

1   growing under a cold frame
Many oriental vegetables can be grown successfully under cover in a temperate climate. A cold frame built on a brick base provides a warm and permanent environment. To build the brick base, first use pegs and string to mark out a rectangular trench 210 x 150 cm (6 ft 10 in x 5 ft) on its outer side, and 25 cm (10 in) wide. Dig down to a depth of 40 cm (16 in) and remove the soil.

2   building the walls
Ram down 13 cm (5 in) of hardcore in the base of the trench; pour and level 10 cm (4 in) of concrete on top. Lay two courses of bricks below ground level.

3   completing the brick enclosure
Build the rear wall so that the top is 60 cm (24 in) above ground level. The front wall should be 43 cm (17 in) above ground level. The side walls should slope between the two. The 'steps' in the top of the side walls can be filled with cement to create a smooth slope.

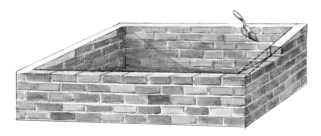

4   assembling the top frame
The top frame should be made from 10 x 5 cm (4 x 2 in) timber, cut to fit exactly the dimensions of the brick enclosure. Join the vertical and horizontal members by sawing out a section from each, half as deep as the timber itself, and as wide as the opposite member.

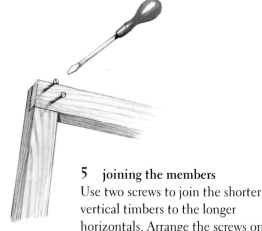

5   joining the members
Use two screws to join the shorter vertical timbers to the longer horizontals. Arrange the screws on the diagonal – if they are in line, they are likely to split the wood.

6   the frame
Treat the frame with preservative, or paint it with primer, undercoat and topcoat. The frame can then be screwed onto the top of the brick enclosure.

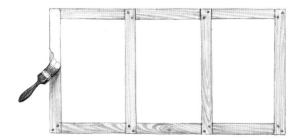

7   attaching battens to the frame
Nail wooden battens 2.5 x 2.5 cm (1 x 1 in) to the shorter cross members. These will prevent the lights (the glazed panels of the cold frame) from sliding sideways when fitted later.

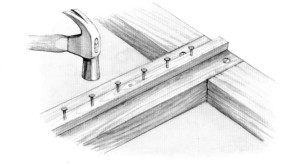

8 making the lights

The simplest lights are rectangular wooden frames that hold a single sheet of glass. The three frames are made from 5 x 5 cm (2 x 2 in) wood, joined at the corners with halved joints, made as described above. The frames should be just wide enough to fit snugly between the vertical battens of the frame – take your measurements carefully from the frame itself.

9 glazing

Using a rebate saw or plane, cut narrow ledges, or rebates, into the edges of the frame to hold the glass. Fit a sheet of horticultural-grade glass that has been cut to the correct size by a glazier. Secure using glazing sprigs and putty.

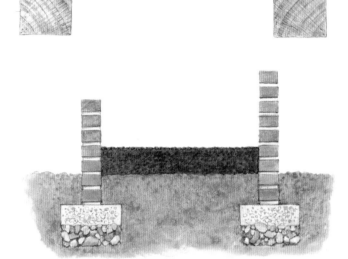

10 planting

Dig the soil at the base of the enclosure, mixing in well-rotted organic material. If this soil is not particularly deep, good garden soil or potting compost can be added on top. Sow seed lengthways across the frame in shallow drills. Stagger the sowings so that crops mature at different times. Thin as necessary.

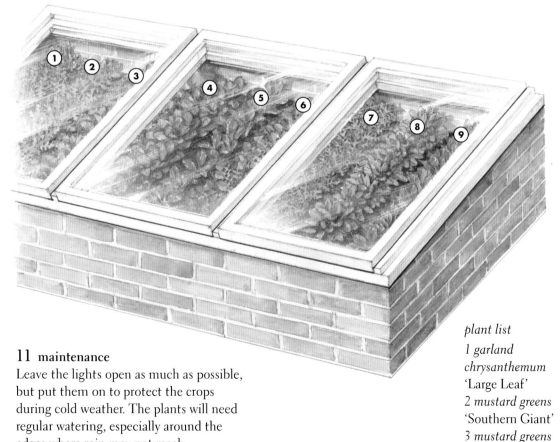

11 maintenance

Leave the lights open as much as possible, but put them on to protect the crops during cold weather. The plants will need regular watering, especially around the edges where rain may not reach.

plant list
1 *garland chrysanthemum* 'Large Leaf'
2 *mustard greens* 'Southern Giant'
3 *mustard greens* 'Red Giant'
4 *pak choi* 'Choki'
5 *Japanese celery*
6 *texsel greens*
7 *garland chrysanthemum* 'Small Leaf'
8 *mustard greens* 'Green in the Snow'
9 *choy sum* 'Purple Flowering'

29

raised vegetable bed

Using raised beds in a vegetable garden is a very old tradition that has recently found favour again. The advantage over conventional beds is that there is an extra depth of good soil, allowing the plants to put their roots down in search of moisture and nutrition. The beds are designed in such a way that they can easily be reached from all sides so that there is no need to walk on and compact the soil – a big advantage.

MATERIALS & EQUIPMENT

bricks • concrete • hardcore • good loam

spade • shovel • spirit level

garden line or pegs and string

tamper • builder's trowel • wheelbarrow

fork • rake • trowel • hoe

seed and plants in variety

well-rotted organic material

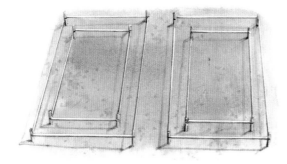

1   planning the beds

Think carefully about the construction of the raised brick beds. They should be just wide enough so that the centre can be reached from either side, and there should be adequate space to move between them. They should be in a sunny but sheltered position.

2   laying the foundations

Dig two trenches forming rectangles 15 cm (6 in) longer and wider than the proposed beds. They should be 25 cm (10 in) wide and 40 cm (16 in) deep. Ram down 13 cm (5 in) of hardcore in the base and then pour and level 10 cm (4 in) of concrete on top of this.

3   building the walls

The walls of the beds are brick; they are easy to construct and look attractive, but they could equally be made of concrete blocks, which are quicker to lay. Build up the walls so that there are two courses below ground and four above – about 30 cm (12 in) higher than the surrounding soil.

allowing for drainage
Once the soil in the bed has been dug, water should drain away easily. But to ensure that no water gets trapped within the walls, a vertical joint should be left uncemented every 45 cm (18 in) when laying the course of bricks at ground level.

4   ground preparation

When the cement has hardened, prepare the bed. Kill or remove all traces of perennial weeds. Dig the soil to at least one spade depth but preferably double-dig it to two, being careful not to bring any subsoil into the top layer. Add plenty of organic material.

5 filling the beds
Once the existing soil in the beds has been cleaned and dug, add a mixture of good quality topsoil (loam) and well-rotted organic material. Fill the beds right up. Do this in autumn and leave over winter for it to weather. Top up with more soil and compost in spring.

6 path between the beds
The area between the beds needs to be kept clear for easy access. To prevent it becoming a mass of weeds or a muddy track, it can be covered with paving slabs.

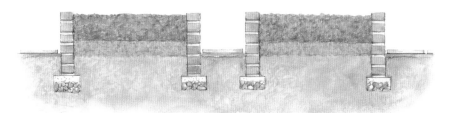

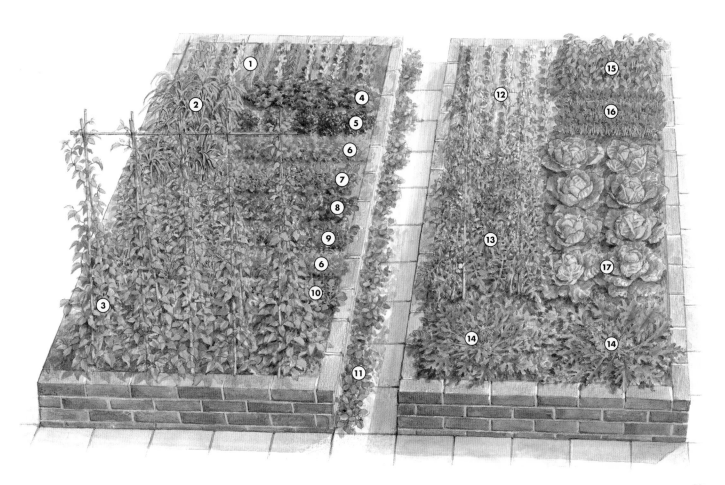

7 planting
Vegetables can be planted in blocks or rows. If you cannot reach directly into the centre of the beds, lay a plank between the rows to walk upon. Left in position, planks will also help keep the weeds down and retain moisture.

plant list

1 seeds	*5 lettuce*	*10 swedes*	*14 courgettes*
2 leeks	*6 carrots*	*11 alpine*	*15 dwarf*
3 runner	*7 turnips*	*strawberries*	*beans*
beans	*8 beetroot*	*12 lettuce*	*16 celery*
4 parsley	*9 parsnips*	*13 tomatoes*	*17 cabbages*

container-grown fruit and vegetables

Growing food for the table is a practical proposition even in the smallest of gardens. Most vegetables, fruit and herbs can be raised in containers as long as they hold sufficient growing medium and are watered at least once a day. The best container crops are those which produce edible leaves or fruit continuously and so do not create gaps in the display when harvested. Plants with coloured fruit – such as tomatoes – or those with ornamental flowers – such as runner beans and courgettes – are worth considering.

left Citrus trees in pots make good specimen plants and can be used, like these orange trees, on either side of a doorway, gateway or steps, or on the patio. They are tender and need moving inside for the winter. Outside they do best in a warm, sheltered position.

below left There is no excuse for tired and limp lettuce when you grow your own in containers on the patio just outside the kitchen door. Cut-and-come-again varieties are best; those with coloured or frilly leaves not only look delightful on the plate but make for highly ornamental pot plants.

above Chillies are ideal plants for pots as they are both decorative and edible. They come in a wide variety of shapes and their glossy colour varies from green to yellow through to red. Their taste also changes with the colour, green being the mildest and red the hottest.

right A collection of pots showing the variety of produce that can be raised. It includes fruit (strawberries), herbs (thyme and oregano) and vegetables (beetroot and potatoes).

right Tomatoes are easy to grow in any type of container from tubs to window boxes or, as here, in hanging baskets. Special trailing forms can be raised to create a decorative as well as productive display.

below Cooks recognize the convenience of keeping fresh herbs close to hand, making them ideal patio pot plants. Many, such as these thymes, are happy in small, shallow pots as long as they are regularly watered.

rooftop kitchen garden

As space becomes increasingly precious, every square inch has to be used to best advantage. Living in a top-floor flat in a city centre seems to preclude any chance of growing vegetables; but by making use of a flat roof, it is possible to create a productive kitchen garden. Restricted access to a roof space means it is easier to build planting containers *in situ* rather than trying to move ready-made structures into place.

MATERIALS & EQUIPMENT

For each bed:

8 lengths of 5 x 5 cm (2 x 2 in) timber, 75 cm (2 ft 6 in) long (legs)

12 planks of 15 cm x 2.5 cm (6 x 1 in), 75 cm (2 ft 6 in) long (legs)

12 planks of 15 x 2.5 cm (6 x 1 in), 90 cm (3 ft) long (sides of beds)

4 planks of 15 x 2.5 cm (6 x 1 in), 60 cm (2 ft) long (ends of beds)

6 sections of 95 x 60 cm (3 ft 2 in x 2 ft) shuttering plywood (floors of beds)

12 lengths of 7.5 x 5 cm (3 x 2 in) wood, 90 cm (3 ft) long (side-bearers)

12 lengths of 7.5 x 5 cm (3 x 2 in) wood, 60 cm (2 ft) long (cross-bearers)

16 lengths of 2.5 x 2.5 cm (1 x 1 in) wood, 30 cm (12 in) long (inner leg rebates)

galvanized screws • wooden trellising

set square • saw • drill • screwdriver • hammer • spirit level • hand fork and trowel

young plants and seed in variety • garden soil • well-rotted organic material

1 assessing the space

Before starting, consult a builder to confirm that the roof can withstand the weight of the garden and will not be damaged by walking and working upon it. On paper, carefully plan out the position of the beds, containers and any furniture needed for the garden, leaving plenty of room to move about. The design of the beds is modular, so the wood can be cut to length on the ground and taken piece by piece to the roof and assembled. Nevertheless, building a rooftop garden is a major undertaking.

2 choosing your vegetables

The rooftop garden shown here centres on two raised beds, each 285 cm (9 ft 6 in) long and 60 cm (2 ft) wide. The beds are 75 cm (30 in) high, allowing for easy access; beneath each bed is a shelf that can be used for holding pots and seed trays. This is just one possible planting scheme.

plant list

1 tomatoes
2 runner beans
3 lettuce
4 basil
5 cabbages
6 radishes
7 spring onions
8 carrots
9 beetroot

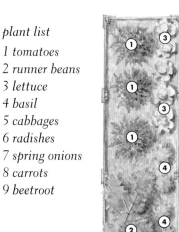
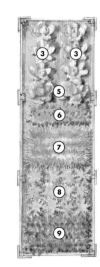

3 making the frame legs

Make the frame of each bed from wood that has been treated with preservative (not creosote). Each of the eight legs consists of a 75 cm (2 ft 6 in) piece of 5 x 5 cm (2 x 2 in) wood. Screw a 15 x 2.5 cm (6 x 1 in) plank to the outside face of each of the four central legs using galvanized screws.

the corner legs
For the four legs at the corners of the bed, screw two 15 x 2.5 cm (6 x 1 in) planks to the outside faces of the leg. The planks provide surfaces to which the side-bearers of the bed can be fixed.

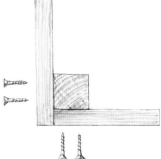

4 attaching the side-bearers

Screw lengths of treated 7.5 x 5 cm (3 x 2 in) timber to the protruding lips of the planks to create the side-bearers, which will support the weight of the soil in the bed and the shelf below. They should be attached so that the upper tier of side-bearers is 45 cm (18 in) above ground level, and the lower tier is 15 cm (6 in) above ground.

5 adding the cross-bearers

To complete the frame, cross-bearers should be fitted. These are 60 cm (2 ft) lengths of treated timber, 7.5 x 5 cm (3 x 2 in) in cross section. Screw these into the side bearers of the lower tier at intervals of about 45 cm (18 in).

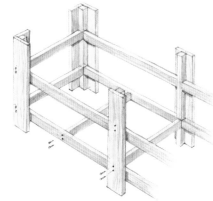

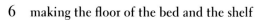

6 making the floor of the bed and the shelf

The lower shelf and base of the raised bed are cut from 2.5 cm (1 in) thick waterproof shuttering plywood. Drill holes at regular intervals to allow water to escape. Starting with the lower shelf, screw the plywood to the side-bearers and cross-bearers. Next, fix cross-bearers to the upper tier and screw on plywood to make the floor of the bed.

7 fitting the leg rebates

The sides of the bed are made from planks that can be slotted in and out of position for easy maintenance. Make a rebate for the planks by screwing lengths of 2.5 x 2.5 cm (1 x 1 in) wood to the leg uprights. This creates a slot wide enough to take a 2.5 cm (1 in) wide plank.

8 slotting in the sides

The 15 x 2.5 cm (6 x 1 in) side and end planks are then cut to length and slotted into position. Two planks, one resting on the other, make a bed 30 cm (12 in) deep.

9 filling the bed

Cover holes in the plywood base of the bed with old pieces of pot so that water can run through, but soil cannot. Cover the base of the bed with small stones. Fill the bed to three quarters maximum depth with good quality loam, or topsoil mixed with garden compost or manure. For deeper-rooted vegetables, fill the bed completely.

10 maintenance

Look after the plants as you would in a conventional bed. Add fresh organic material periodically. This may necessitate the removal of some existing compost, although this will shrink as it breaks down. Every three years, empty the beds and treat the timber with a non-toxic preservative.

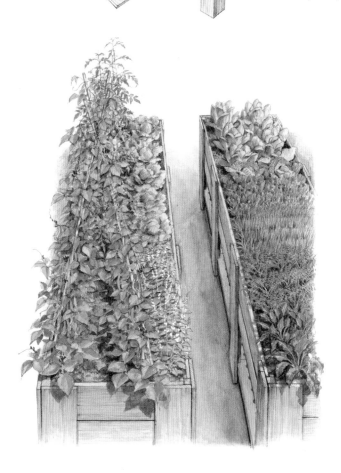

basket of tomatoes

In a small garden, every square inch can be exploited to produce vegetables. Vertical space can be filled using hanging baskets and window boxes; and with careful choice of plants, the baskets can be attractive as well as productive. Here tomatoes have been mixed with flowering and foliage plants, but they can equally be grown alongside other vegetables if space allows. Several baskets in a group, hung at different heights, make an impressive display.

MATERIALS & EQUIPMENT

basket • liner

galvanized eye and hook • compost

slow-release fertilizer or liquid feed

basket waterer • trowel • secateurs

1 tomato 'Tumbler'

2 petunia (*Petunia* 'Purple')

2 variegated plectranthus (*Plectranthus coleoides* 'Variegatus')

1 preparing the basket

Hanging baskets are available in a range of materials and designs. Wire baskets are inexpensive and light, but wrought iron, terracotta, wicker or wooden baskets may be preferred for aesthetic reasons. Before a basket can be filled and planted, it must be lined.

2 lining

Fit the lining, which may be of fibre, moulded paper, moss or polythene; the last is ugly if not completely covered by plants. The lining is likely to be porous, so drainage is not a problem. It is easier to work on the basket if it is supported on a bucket, particularly if a heavier basket is used.

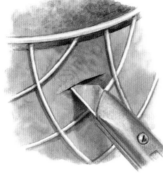

3 filling the basket

Hanging vegetable baskets look their best when completely covered with plants, so it helps to plant the sides as well as the top. Use a craft knife to cut holes or slits in the liner before pouring in the compost. Make the holes no bigger than necessary to push the plant through.

4 planting the sides

Partly fill the basket with compost to just below the level of the slits in the lining. Wrap the roots of the petunia plants in damp tissue to prevent damage, then push the young plants through the holes in the lining, spreading their roots. Fill the basket with compost. Petunias make a decorative display, but productive plants such as lettuces can be substituted.

5 planting the tomato

Plant the tomato in the centre of the basket, so that it will hang down on all sides. One of the best tomatoes to use is a variety called 'Tumbler', which has been specially developed for planting in hanging baskets.

6 hanging

Baskets with tomatoes should be hung in a warm, sunny position. If there is an existing beam, then a stout eye screwed into the woodwork will be enough support. Be certain to ensure that the beam is strong and in good repair. The basket can be hung at any height that seems appropriate. Lower is easier for care and maintenance, but baskets usually look best when above eye-level.

7 watering and feeding

Hanging a basket above head height makes watering difficult. One solution is to use a pump-action water dispenser with a long, bent lance. Unless it is raining, baskets should be watered at least once a day; twice on hot days. They also need regular feeding. A slow-release fertilizer can be incorporated in the compost, or liquid feed can be added to the water. Harvest fruit as it ripens and remove any that is damaged or over-ripe.

8 grouping baskets

Vegetable baskets look especially attractive in groups of three or more. Hang them at different heights for the best effect. For variety, hang one basket below another.

salad basket
As an alternative to tomatoes, plant the basket with cut-and-come-again lettuces. There are varieties available with red foliage and with crinkly and oak leaf-shaped leaves. A surprising number can be included in the basket if planted round the sides as well as on top. The result will be a ball of colourful lettuce.

43

patio container garden

Even the smallest paved patio can be transformed into a kitchen garden. Anywhere that provides a small area for standing containers is enough to produce a few crops. Quantities may be a bit restricted but the quality of fresh home-grown produce will be abundantly apparent. As well as producing vegetables, fruit and herbs, a patio kitchen garden will be an attractive feature if well designed. Virtually any fruit or vegetable can be grown, although the less rampant varieties are preferred.

MATERIALS & EQUIPMENT

variety of terracotta pots

potting compost

broken crocks or stones

60 x 5 cm (2 ft x 2 in) plastic drainpipe

pick axe • spade • fork

trowel • secateurs • drill

plants in variety

1   preparing for planting

The average paved patio provides many opportunities for planting crops for the table. Conventional terracotta pots are attractive, versatile and free-draining; larger containers can be made from half-barrels; and many vegetables thrive in grow-bags. Spreading plants are best planted directly into the ground: use a pick axe to lift a few of the paving slabs.

2   ground plants

Remove any rubble and sand from beneath the lifted slabs. Break up the soil below this and then fill the remaining space with fresh soil or compost. Plant spreading herbs such as thyme and marjoram and water well.

3   pot plants

Most vegetables will grow well in pots, even small containers. Crock the bottom of the pot and fill with a good, fresh compost. Sow the seed thinly on the top and cover with a thin layer of compost. Cover the pot with netting to prevent birds or animals from disturbing the compost.

4   strawberry pot

There are several types of strawberry pot available; the most decorative are tall terracotta towers that have planting holes in the sides as well as on top. Strawberry towers are also available in plastic.

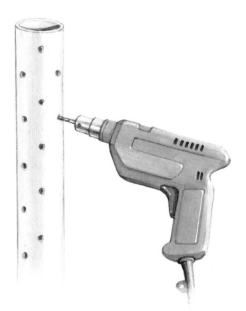

5   irrigation pipe

Tall strawberry pots are difficult to water right to the bottom, but it is easy to make a simple device to ensure they are well irrigated. Buy a length of 5 cm (2 in) diameter plastic pipe (drainpipe will do). Drill three 3 mm (⅛ in) holes around the pipe at 5 cm (2 in) intervals along its length.

6 making up the pot

Place the pipe in the centre of the pot and fill around it with compost until you reach the first hole in the side of the pot. Place the strawberry roots through the hole and continue to fill with compost until the next hole is reached. Plant further strawberries until the pot is filled.

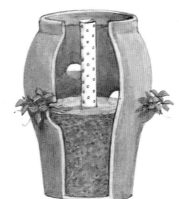

7 watering the strawberry pot

Fill up the pipe with water, and water the top of the pot. If the bottom of the tube is not in tight contact with the bottom of the pot, the water may run out too quickly. If this is the case, slow down its release by ramming a ball of crumpled polythene down the tube. This will slow the flow sufficiently to allow water to percolate out of the side holes. Water the pot regularly so that it never dries out.

8 care and maintenance

Water the pots every day and feed with a liquid feed once a week. Keep the plants neat, · removing diseased individuals on sight. Harvest vegetables and fruit as required; avoid leaving over-ripe and rotting produce on the plants.

plant list

1 lemon balm	6 carrots	9 gooseberries	14 lettuce
2 rosemary	7 bush	10 patio rose	15 potatoes
3 lemon verbena	tomatoes	11 beetroot	16 courgettes
4 runner beans	8 cordon	12 strawberries	17 marjoram
5 sage	tomatoes	13 leeks	18 pear tree

fruit trees in pots

Fruit is usually associated with large bushes or even huge trees, but most
varieties have dwarf forms that grow well in containers; there are even apple trees
that can be grown as patio plants. However, it is the more exotic fruit, such as oranges
and lemons, that are especially good for using in containers. This is partly because
they are easier to look after if they can be moved in and out of doors, but also
because their fruit and foliage are very decorative.

MATERIALS & EQUIPMENT

terracotta pots

stones for drainage

potting compost

slow-release fertilizer or liquid feed

secateurs

young fruit trees

1 selecting pots

Pots should be considered from a practical as well as aesthetic perspective. Plastic pots are much lighter than terracotta but are easier to over-water and provide less thermal insulation for a plant's roots in winter. Terracotta pots look better with the Mediterranean fruit trees used here. They are cooler in summer and warmer in winter, and are heavier than plastic, which means that they are less likely to fall over in a wind; however, they are more difficult to move when full of compost.

2 planting the trees

Crock the bottom of the pots well to aid drainage. Partly fill with compost; place the plant in and fill up to the top. Firm down and water.

3 choosing a position

While most exotic fruit trees need winter protection, they can be placed outside during the summer. They are best positioned against a south-facing wall. This not only provides a good backdrop, but also acts as a storage heater at night. Placing them in a corner offers even better protection. Avoid locations overshadowed by other buildings or trees, or those which funnel draughts over the trees. Containers should be watered every day, and at least twice on hot days or when there is a drying wind. A liquid feed can be added to the water once a month.

4 potting on

The plants used are all perennials and so need to be potted on every year into larger pots until they reach their maximum size. Remove them from their existing pot and shake off any loose compost around the root ball. As the plants get towards their maximum size, some of the roots can be trimmed back. Repot into a pot one size larger using fresh compost and water well.

5 the fruiting plants

In temperate climates, oranges, lemons and limes can be grown purely as ornamentals, but they will fruit if given enough warmth. To maximize fruiting in cooler areas, the plants, in their pots, should be kept in a greenhouse or conservatory to provide them with extra warmth.

plant list: fruit trees
1 *Calamondin orange*
(Citrofortunella
microcarpa)
2 *Natal plum*
(Carissa grandiflora)
3 *Meyer's lemon*
(Citrus meyeri 'Meyer')
4 *variegated lemon*
(Citrus limon
'Variegata')

additional plants
A few pots of smaller plants will act as fillers around the edge of the group; climbers provide a backdrop for the group.

5 *assorted low-growing ornamentals*
6 *rosemary*
(Rosmarinus officinalis)
7 *wisteria*
(Wisteria floribunda)

6 winter care

Most exotic fruit trees and bushes are not winter hardy and so need to be moved under cover – a warm greenhouse or conservatory is ideal. The plants should be kept inside until all possible threat of frost has passed and the daytime temperature reaches an average of 20°C (68°F). Be careful not to over-water during the winter – just keep the soil barely moist.

alternative fruit tree arrangement
Less exotic fruits are hardier and can be left outside as long as their containers do not freeze solid. Protect the containers by wrapping straw or bubble wrap around them when cold weather is forecast. Remove the wrapping in warm weather.

1 *pole apple*
2 *standard gooseberry*
3 *blueberry*
4 *strawberry tower*
5 *rosemary*
6 *additional plants (as above)*

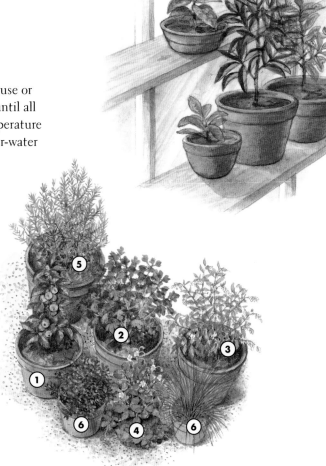

chillies in pots

Of all vegetables, chillies are perhaps the most suitable for growing in pots.
They make a spectacular display, as well as providing spice for the kitchen. There
is a wide range of varieties available that produce yellow, orange, red or purple fruit
in bushes of different sizes; in some cultivars, the chillies hang from the branches
and in others they are borne upright. Chillies grow slowly in temperate climates;
the first fruits will appear about 15 weeks after planting.

MATERIALS & EQUIPMENT

seed trays • sowing compost

7.5 cm (3 in) pots for seedlings

large terracotta pots • broken pieces of pot

potting compost • watering can

high-potash liquid feed

chilli plants in variety or seed of several varieties

1 chilli varieties

Chillies are branching perennials that can grow to a height of 1.5 m (5 ft). They are sub-tropical plants and will not tolerate frosts or low temperatures. Therefore they must be started off in a greenhouse or conservatory and not placed outside until the threat of frost has passed. The different varieties of chillies vary in size and shape. They start green but redden as they ripen. The riper they are, the hotter they become.

2 growing from seed

If you cannot obtain young plants, chillies may be grown from seed, which is more readily available. Sow the seed in trays in early to mid-spring and place in a warm spot or propagator at about 21°C (70°F). Don't let the seed dry out. If in a propagator, there should be no need to water.

3 potting the seedlings

When large enough to handle, prick the plants out into individual pots and grow on in a warm environment. Avoid placing the pots in a cold draught and beware of frost.

4 containers

Terracotta pots are perfect for growing chillies; ideally, use pots that are less than about 45 cm (18 in) across because they are light enough to be moved inside during cooler weather. The pots must have a hole in the bottom to allow excess water to drain away.

5 repotting

Once the plants are about 10 cm (4 in) high, plant them into their final pots. Crock the bottom of the pot with stones or broken pot; fill with a good quality compost and plant the chilli. Water well. If using large pots, place them in their final position before filling with compost; moist compost adds greatly to the weight.

6   pinching out

When the plants reach a height of about 15 cm (6 in), pinch off their growing tops to make them bush out. Chillies need a sheltered site and should be placed against a south-facing wall, which will radiate heat during the night, helping to keep the plants warm. Plants should be taken indoors if the temperature drops below 18°C (65°F). Sweet peppers will tolerate slightly cooler conditions and can be used as a substitute.

7   displaying, watering and feeding

If the plants you have chosen are about the same height, use some form of staging – such as bricks or inverted pots – to vary the level. This will display the plants to best effect and let light through to the plants at the back. The plants will need watering every day and perhaps twice a day in very hot weather. High-potash liquid feed should be added to the water every 10 days once the fruit has started to swell.

8   harvesting

The fruit can be picked as soon as it is large enough. It can be picked at the green stage when it will be at its mildest or at its final coloured stage (red, yellow or purple) when it will be hotter. Pick the chillies with part of the stalk still attached. Be certain to have picked all the fruit, or have moved the plants inside, before the first frosts.

climbing fruit and vegetables

above Although hops are perennials, they die back to the ground each year. These dense twining plants are perfect for growing up trellis to create a backdrop to the vegetable garden.

Many people see the vegetable garden as a flat utilitarian area of planting, but a far more interesting scene can be created by adding height to the beds using permanent objects, such as fruit trees grown against walls or forming walkways, or other decorative features. Climbing annuals, including runner beans and trailing marrows, can also be used to great effect. They can be grown up temporary supports, such as cane wigwams, or trail over more permanent structures, such as a metal archways or arbours. Carefully chosen, the structures themselves can add vertical interest to the garden throughout the year.

left Grape vines are decorative, productive and can help utilize space in the garden that would otherwise go unfilled. Vines are also useful for covering eyesores such as garages and oil storage tanks.

below Pears, like most other fruit trees, can be trained in ways to suit the small garden. Full-size trees may be out of the question, but cordons like this, for example, take up very little space.

right Apples and pears can
be trained in many ways.
A decorative method suitable
for use in the kitchen garden
is to train them over iron
frameworks to form walkways
or arbours.

right Cordon tomatoes can
be trained up canes in the
main beds or supported by
fences. While bush tomatoes
are more practical because
they do not need staking,
they are not as attractive.

left Grape vines need not
be grown in a controlled
manner on conventional
wirework. They can be allowed
to ramble over arches to make
shady paths and sitting areas.

below Beans provide a
strong vertical element in
the kitchen garden. They
can be grown up a variety of
frameworks, including rows
or wigwams of canes, or poles,
strings or netting.

pear tunnel

A pergola or archway covered with pears is a romantic addition to the garden, and provides a good crop as well as decorative interest throughout the year. In the winter there is the tracery of the bare branches to be admired. In spring, pure white blossom covers the arches. In the heat of summer the leaves provide a cool, shady walkway. In autumn there is, of course, the fruit to be enjoyed and, finally, the blaze of colour as the foliage takes on its autumn tints before dropping.

MATERIALS & EQUIPMENT

proprietary or custom-made steel pergola

galvanized wire

2 straining bolts per horizontal wire

bolts to connect the tops of the curved metal uprights

pegs and string • rubble • builder's sand • gravel

7.5 x 1 cm (3 x ½ in) edging boards

plant ties

spade • shovel

spanner to fit straining bolts

spanner to fit bolts on uprights

garden roller • secateurs

2 maiden whip pear trees per 45 cm (18 in) of tunnel

well-rotted organic material

1 choosing a framework

Tunnels for carrying fruit trees are available 'off the peg', but it's best to have one made to your specifications by a blacksmith or workshop. The simplest tunnel is no more than a line of metal arches. Each arch is made from two curved posts bolted together at the apex; the posts have holes along their length through which wires can be run. Here, the posts are steel, about 6 mm (¼ in) thick and 4 cm (2 in) wide.

2 laying out the plan

When planning the tunnel, don't forget that the branches and fruit will hang down within, so allow plenty of space to walk through. Lay out the plan of the walkway, marking the position of the leg of each arch with pegs set 90 cm (3 ft) apart. Use shorter pegs and string to mark the path and beds to be planted.

3 securing the posts

Dig a hole 45–60 cm (18–24 in) deep and about 30 cm (12 in) square for each upright and tip in about 13 cm (5 in) of rubble. Place the leg in position and fill the hole with concrete. Before the concrete sets, check with a spirit level that the post is vertical, and that it meets the opposite side of the arch. Bolt the two halves of the arch together.

4 horizontal supports

When the concrete has set, thread galvanized wire through holes in the posts to form horizontal supports. Pull the wire as tight as possible and then connect each end to a straining bolt. Tighten the bolts so that the wires have no slack left in them.

5 laying a path

To lay a gravel path through the tunnel, first excavate the area to a depth of 20 cm (8 in). Lay treated edging boards around the perimeter of the dug area. Fill with 10 cm (4 in) of hard core. Compact the rubble and cover with 5 cm (2 in) of sand. Compact the sand with a roller and top up with 3–5 cm (1–2 in) of gravel, rolling it in several layers.

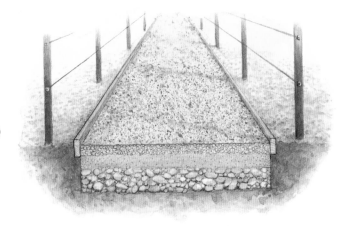

6   planting the pear trees
Plant the trees at 45 cm (18 in) intervals. At each
planting site, thoroughly dig the soil and add as
much well-rotted compost as possible. The best time
for planting is between late autumn and early spring.
Set the plants in the ground so that the top of the
rootball is level with the surface of the soil. Firm
them in and water.

7   pruning
When planted 45 cm (18 in) apart, the
trees are trained as cordons (each cordon
is basically a single stem with short laterals
on each side). Reduce the laterals to about
three leaves when planting and cut back
any new laterals to the same amount each
summer. New growth on old laterals should
be pruned back to one leaf.

8   finished arch
After a few years, the leaders will meet
at the top of the arch; new growth should
then be restricted to one bud. Keep the
trees pruned or they will rapidly become
overgrown. Harvest the pears as soon as
they ripen; they are ready as soon as they
come away easily by twisting the fruit.

bean arbour

A seat beneath a flower-laden arbour is a feature associated with formal ornamental gardens, but there is no reason why such a decorative refuge cannot be incorporated into the kitchen garden. Covered with runner beans, the arbour can be both beautiful and productive. It is possible to create a permanent structure or something more temporary, which can be moved from one year to the next.

MATERIALS & EQUIPMENT

proprietary arbour framework

pegs and string • rubble

treated edging boards 23 cm (9 in) wide, 2 cm (¾ in) deep

coarse gravel • sand • pea gravel • concrete

spade • shovel • trowel • rake

garden roller • tamper

4 scarlet runner bean plants, *Phaseolus coccineus*, per metre (3 ft)

well-rotted organic material

1   selecting an arbour
Choose an arbour frame from a garden centre or mail
order supplier, or find a blacksmith who will produce a
more unusual design to your specifications. Think carefully
about size – you may wish to fit a table as well as a bench
under the arbour – and you should allow about 30 cm
(12 in) for growth of the runner beans within the frame.

2   preparing the ground
Clear the area of ground on which you want
to place the arbour. Peg out the position of
the arbour legs, and use further pegs and
string to mark out the edges of a seating
area and approaching path, both of which
will be laid with gravel for durability.

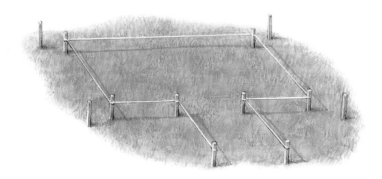

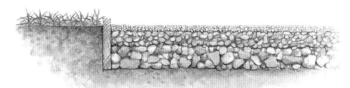

3   excavating the base
In the seating and path area, dig down to a
depth of 20 cm (8 in) and remove the soil.
Place treated boards around the dug area,
securing with wooden pegs at 1 m (3 ft)
intervals. Use a heavy roller to flatten the base.

4   laying the path and base
Cover the base of the excavated area with hardcore to a depth of
10 cm (4 in). Lay a middle layer of coarse gravel and sand 5 cm
(2 in) deep, and cover this with 2.5 cm (1 in) of pea gravel. Rake
the surface to level off.

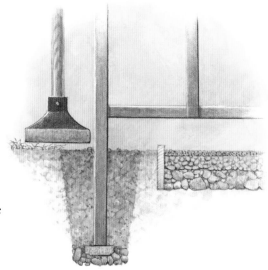

5   securing the arbour
In sheltered sites, you don't need to concrete in the uprights
of the arbour frame. Dig a hole for each post at least 45 cm
(18 in) deep. Add a 10 cm (4 in) layer of gravel and place the
framework in position. Refill the holes, ramming down the
earth firmly with a tamper. In exposed sites, it is best to
concrete the framework into position because wind pressure
on the plant-covered arbour can be significant.

6 planting and watering

After the threat of frost has passed, dig the soil around the arbour and plant the runner beans. Plant a seedling against each post and then at 25 cm (10 in) intervals. Scatter slug pellets around the base. Water thoroughly.

7 training the beans

Beans will naturally twine up and over the arbour but it may be necessary to direct them at the initial stages to ensure that there is even coverage. There is no need to tie the stems – it is enough just to tuck them in.

8 arbour in bloom

Don't let the beans dry out, especially once the flowers have started to form. To encourage bushier growth, pinch out the tops of the stems when they reach the middle of the arbour. The beans produce a display of red, pink or white flowers, depending on variety.

9 harvesting the beans

Pick the beans when about 15 cm (6 in) long. It is best to harvest every 3–4 days, taking the beans before their seeds swell. Don't leave old pods on the plants; they inhibit the formation of new ones.

wall-trained redcurrants

Redcurrants are a neglected fruit in the garden. This is surprising because they
have a deliciously fresh taste that is a treat whether they are eaten from the bush
or as part of a dish. Culinary benefits aside, redcurrants are also very attractive plants.
When grown in conventional bushes, they have a certain appealing quality, but they
are at their best when trained against a wall. Whitecurrants and gooseberries
can be grown to spectacular effect in the same way.

MATERIALS & EQUIPMENT

wall plugs • galvanized wire

vine eyes and straining bolt

2 garden canes per plant

plant ties

drill with masonry bit • hammer

pliers • spade and secateurs

redcurrant plants

well-rotted organic material

1 supporting the redcurrant plant

The bush will need some form of support against the wall. The best way of securing it, especially if several bushes are to be grown, is to use vine eyes that hammer or screw into the wall, through which galvanized wire is threaded and secured. The wires should be about 45 cm (18 in) apart and the supporting vine eyes at 90 cm (3 ft) intervals.

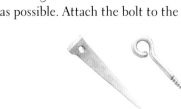

2 fixing the wires

Thread the wire through the vine eyes. Fasten the wire at one end using pliers to twist it back on itself. Use a straining bolt at the other end to make the wire as taut as possible. Attach the bolt to the wall through a vine eye.

3 choosing a plant

Choose a redcurrant bush with two strong shoots coming from the rootstock. If there are more, remove the extra ones with a pair of secateurs, cutting as close to the base as possible. If there is only one main shoot, choose a plant with a strong, low-down side shoot. Thoroughly prepare the ground in which the currant is to be planted by removing any perennial weeds and incorporating plenty of manure.

vine eyes
These galvanized fasteners come in various shapes. Some are nailed into the wall; others screw into wall plugs.

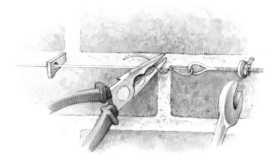

4 planting

Plant the bush a little way out from the wall. It should be at the same depth in the soil as it was in its original container. Fasten two canes vertically to the wires, making paths along which the currant can be trained. Tie in the two main stems, one to each cane. Remove any side shoots back to one bud.

5 pruning

As the two main stems grow, tie them in to the canes, removing any new side shoots back to the first bud. Completely remove any shoots below 25 cm (10 in) on the main stems.

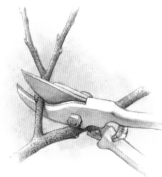

climbing alternatives

three-stem cordon
Gooseberries, redcurrants and whitecurrants can be grown
in three-stemmed cordons. The method is basically the same
as described for the double cordon, except that the central,
as well as two side shoots, are retained.

fan planting
Currants can be trained into a fan, making a spectacular
display against a wall. The best fruits are produced in
sunny, sheltered spots, but redcurrants can thrive against
north-facing walls.

redcurrant fence
Trained redcurrants can liven up tired wooden fences,
trellising or even open wirework. Bushes can be grown to
a height of 2 m (6 ft), and produce a crop of about 1 kg
(2.2 lb) of fruit per year over a period of 10–12 years.

6   maintenance and training
Every summer cut back any side shoots to 4–5 leaves. In the winter
reduce these shoots even further, back to 1–2 buds. Follow these
simple pruning procedures annually to maximize fruit yield. Once the
two main leaders have reached the height you want, cut out the tips.

apple arch

A kitchen garden can be much more than a two-dimensional planting.
The best designs make full use of the available area and height to maximize
productivity and decorative impact. Certain vegetables, such as runner beans,
add dimension to the garden, but ideally, more permanent features should be
incorporated to define the space. An apple arch in the centre of the garden where
paths meet adds a touch of elegance as well as permanence to the garden.

MATERIALS & EQUIPMENT

proprietary arch or

8 lengths of 3.5 m (11½ ft) x 1 cm (½ in) steel rod

4 lengths of 4.6 m (15 ft) x 1 cm (½ in) steel rod

20 cm (8 in) length of copper water pipe

galvanized wire

paint (metal primer, undercoat and topcoat)

concrete • string or plant ties

spade • shovel • spirit level • set square

hacksaw • pliers • secateurs

4 feathered-maiden apple trees

well-rotted organic material

1 planning

Arches can be bought 'off the shelf', but it is easy to make one from 1 cm (½ in) steel rod usually used for concrete reinforcing. When choosing an arch framework, be generous with size – an arch 2 m (6½ ft) tall will have a clearance of just 1.7 m (5½ ft) once covered with the tree. First, use pegs to mark the positions of the arch's legs in the corners of a plot 2.2 x 2.2 m (7 x 7 ft). Use a set square and strings to check that it is a perfect square.

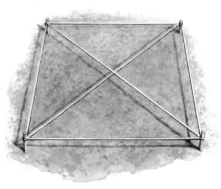

2 home-made framework

Each of the four legs of the arch is made from three steel rods. Using a hacksaw, cut two 3.5 m (11½ ft) lengths and one 4.6 m (15 ft) length. Bind the three rods together with wire up to a height of 1.8 m (6 ft) so that they form a single column.

3 preparing the foundations

At the foot of each of the four legs, dig a hole 45 cm (18 in) deep and 30 cm (12 in) wide. Ram rubble into the base to a depth of about 10 cm (4 in).

4 setting in the legs

Place each leg into a dug hole. Carefully check that the leg is upright using a spirit level. Fill the hole with concrete to set in the legs. Ensure that the long steel rod of each leg faces into the middle of the arch before pouring the concrete and allowing it to set.

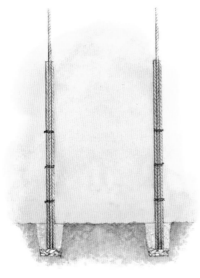

5 forming the arches

Once the concrete has set, bend each rod over to meet its 'opposite number'. Try to keep the curves as even as possible. The short rods bend to make the perimeter of the arch, while the long rods bend to meet in the middle of the arch to form its 'roof'.

6 securing the arches

Where two rods meet they can either be bound with wire or secured by using a 20 cm (8 in) length of copper water pipe as a sleeve to hold them together. The rods may need to be cut to their final length with a hacksaw before the sleeve is fitted.

7 completing the structure

Protect the steel rods by applying a metal primer, undercoat and a topcoat of paint. This not only gives the frame a good finish but also helps prevent rusting. The arch works well as the centrepiece of a garden; if needed, lay gravel paths running through the arch, as described on page 60.

8 planting

Plant an apple tree at each corner of the arch. Dig a hole deeper and wider than the rootball. Add some compost and dig it into the base of the hole. Mix more compost with the remaining soil and use this to refill the hole. Plant the trees at the same depth as they were in their pots and water well. Allow the main shoot to grow up the poles, tying it in as it grows. Reduce the side shoots to three leaves or three buds.

9 training side shoots

When the main stem grows past the point where the legs divide, allow two side shoots to develop, tying them in as they grow. Again reduce any new side shoots to three leaves and cut back material on older growth to one leaf.

10 maintenance

Prune in winter and summer, cutting back any new side shoots to three leaves, while pruning the new growth on older material back to one leaf. Pick the fruit when ripe for eating, or when firm but just under-ripe for storage. Wrap each fruit in grease-proof paper, and store in a well-ventilated container in a cool, dark place.

decorative beds and borders

While the main purpose of a kitchen garden is to provide tasty produce for year-round use at the table, it is easy to create a plot that will satisfy the eye as well as the palette. Evergreen herbs can be used to provide interest across the seasons, and many vegetables, such as Swiss chard, with its brilliant red stems, are just as comfortable in a flower border as in a vegetable patch. Old-fashioned kitchen gardens often contained flowers, including pot marigolds, which can still be used to add points of bright colour to the garden.

above Shrubby herbs, such as this permanent, evergreen sage *Salvia officinalis* 'Icterina', provide a backbone to the decorative kitchen garden.

below Fruit trees provide a very decorative element in any kitchen garden. They can be used as standard trees or bushes, but become even more interesting when trained over metal frameworks to become archways, walkways or even low hedges.

top The sages, *Salvia officinalis*, are useful herbs in the kitchen. The purple-leaved 'Purpurascens' mixes well with ornamental plants. It is seen here with the silver-leaved *Stachys byzantina*.

above Fruit trees have several decorative phases. Leaf burst is a welcome sign of spring; in summer their shapes provide vertical interest; and in autumn there is fruit and colourful foliage to enjoy.

right Lettuces are available in a huge range of leaf shapes and colours. Frilly-leaved and red-hued varieties are particularly attractive. Salad onions provide a contrasting leaf shape in the salad bed.

right Flowers, such as pot marigolds (*Calendula officinalis*) also find use in the kitchen. Their petals can be added to salads or used as a substitute for saffron.

below A potager is, strictly speaking, simply a kitchen garden, but the term is increasingly used to describe an ordered, decorative plot that also provides food for the kitchen. Here fruit trees, scented flowers, paths and, of course, vegetables are combined to stunning effect.

fruit among the flowers

Fruit trees and bushes are permanent features in the garden. When in blossom or fruit they are very decorative in their own right, and if trained as standards they add a sculptural quality to the garden. At some times of the year they may become a bit dull, but the plot can be brightened up by planting flowers around their bases to create a scene that changes throughout the seasons.

MATERIALS & EQUIPMENT

spade • fork • rake • trowel

garden line or pegs and string

secateurs • shears

2 standard gooseberry bushes

corn marigold (*Chrysanthemum segetum*) seed

love-in-a-mist (*Nigella damascena*) seed

1 *Geranium endressii*

6 box plants (*Buxus sempervirens* 'Suffruticosa') per metre (3 ft) of hedging

1 planning

Fruit trees and bushes take several years to mature, so any mistakes you make in the design will be slow to rectify. Carefully plan your planting scheme on paper before transferring it to the ground. Use a grid of canes and strings to help with the layout on the ground if necessary.

2 the hedge

Planting a box hedge (see page 24) around the plot makes it a self-contained entity and helps neaten the bed by preventing plants from flopping onto the adjacent path. Use a garden line to ensure that the hedge is planted in a straight line. When mature, it should be trimmed at least once a year.

3 the standard gooseberries

Gooseberry bushes can be bought ready-trained into standards, but it is cheaper and more fun to train your own. This is done by grafting the chosen fruiting variety onto *Ribes odoratum* rootstock. Buy and plant a *Ribes odoratum*. Mulch with well-rotted manure. Select one stem to train vertically and prune back the lateral branches. The plant will be ready to accept a graft in about three years.

4 under-planting

Both annuals and perennials can be planted around the growing gooseberry bushes. Corn marigolds, which are self-sowing (and so save time and energy), work particularly well when mixed with love-in-a-mist and perennial geraniums. The latter should be cut to the ground after flowering to encourage a late flush of foliage and some late flowers.

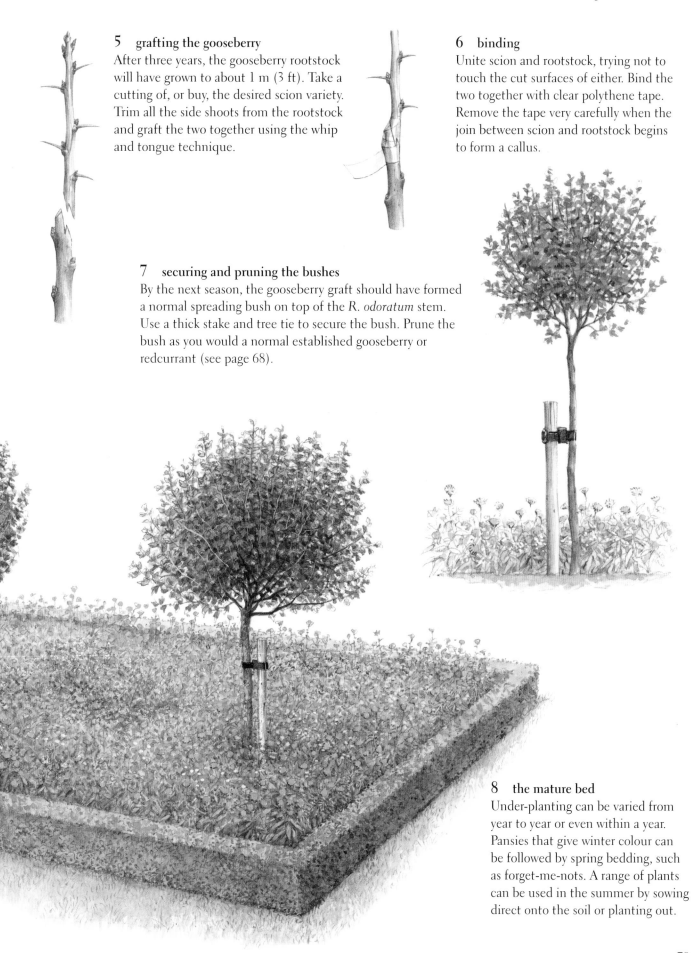

5   grafting the gooseberry
After three years, the gooseberry rootstock will have grown to about 1 m (3 ft). Take a cutting of, or buy, the desired scion variety. Trim all the side shoots from the rootstock and graft the two together using the whip and tongue technique.

6   binding
Unite scion and rootstock, trying not to touch the cut surfaces of either. Bind the two together with clear polythene tape. Remove the tape very carefully when the join between scion and rootstock begins to form a callus.

7   securing and pruning the bushes
By the next season, the gooseberry graft should have formed a normal spreading bush on top of the *R. odoratum* stem. Use a thick stake and tree tie to secure the bush. Prune the bush as you would a normal established gooseberry or redcurrant (see page 68).

8   the mature bed
Under-planting can be varied from year to year or even within a year. Pansies that give winter colour can be followed by spring bedding, such as forget-me-nots. A range of plants can be used in the summer by sowing direct onto the soil or planting out.

decorative vegetable garden

In many modern potagers, the planting is so regimented that harvesting just a single lettuce leaves a gap that spoils the appearance of the whole plot. But it is possible to create a more practical working garden that is highly decorative and yet is not a slave to precision planting. The attractions of this garden come from its overall composition and surroundings; indeed much interest is generated by the irregularity and variation of the crops.

MATERIALS & EQUIPMENT

280 pavoirs or bricks

36 paving slabs 60 x 60 cm (2 x 2 ft)

16 trellis panels 1.8 x 1.8 m (6 x 6 ft)

2 trellis panels 90 cm x 1.8 m (3 x 6 ft)

20 treated wooden posts 10 cm x 10 cm x 2.5 m (4 in x 4 in x 8 ft)

galvanized nails • 2 cu m (2 cu yd) sand

0.2 cu m (7 cu ft) rubble • 1 cu m (1 cu yd) concrete

decorative urn • 12 garden canes 2.5 m (8 ft) long

spade, fork and trowel • tamper • saw and hammer

spirit level • wheelbarrow • garden line or pegs and string

seed and plants in variety

1 planning

Carrying out the hard landscaping is a major task that needs careful planning. First draw up all the elements on squared paper – this will make it easier to transfer your plan to the ground. At this stage, also draw up a plant list to help you ensure that you can get the seedlings or seeds in good time.

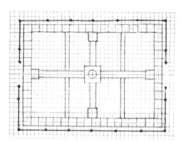

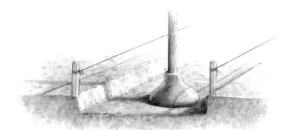

2 preparing the ground

Use pegs and string to mark out the position of the paving and bricks to be laid on the ground. The slabs do not need to be set in concrete; simply ram down the earth within the marked lines as firmly as possible with a tamper.

3 laying the paving

Put down a layer of sand 2.5–5 cm (1–2 in) deep and set the slabs and brick on this, making certain that they are level and firm. Plain natural-coloured paving slabs look best in a vegetable garden.

4 erecting the trellising

The plot is surrounded by rustic trellising on which decorative climbers and fruiting trees are grown. To ensure that the trellis is secure enough to take the considerable load, especially when the wind is blowing, the uprights should be cemented in the ground. The panels can be nailed or screwed to the uprights. Treat the uprights and the trellis panels with a wood preservative (not creosote).

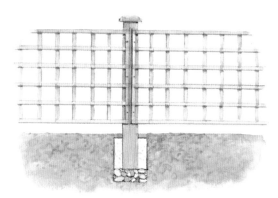

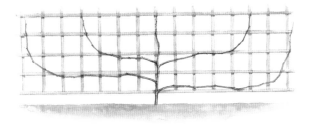

5 planting hops

Hops are highly decorative plants to grow on the trellises; they are of practical use only if you brew your own beer. When buying, ensure that you have a female plant, because the male does not bear fruit. Plant at the same depth as it was in the pot. In spring, spread the young shoots out along the trellis so that the plant covers a wide area. In autumn, cut right back to the ground and remove all the old growth.

6 bean wigwam

Runner beans can be grown up a conventional bean row or in a 'wigwam', which takes up less space. Push 2.5 m (8 ft) canes or poles into the ground so that their bases form a circle. The bases of the canes should be about 30 cm (12 in) apart. They should all be sloped slightly towards the centre of the circle so that the tops all meet. Bundle the tops together and tie tightly with string.

7 planting

The planting can be changed from year to year; for the best effect, mix plants that you use most in the kitchen with some ornamentals. The design of the garden benefits from sparing use of architectural features – here a stone urn.

plant list
1 *vines*
2 *hops*
3 *cordon apples*
4 *spinach*
5 *carrots*
6 *lettuce*
7 *ornamental kale*
8 *beetroot*
9 *parsley*
10 *runner beans*
11 *chives*
12 *courgettes*
13 *Welsh onions*
14 *endive*
15 *parsnips*
16 *tomatoes*

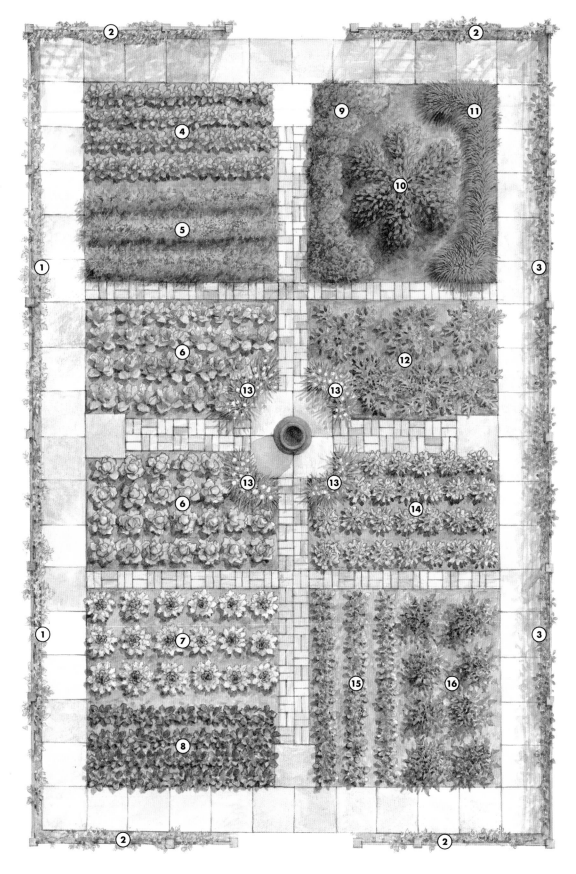

step-over apple hedge

Gone are the days when growing apples meant large trees taking up precious areas of garden space. Now they can be grown in all manner of innovative ways suitable for the smaller garden. The step-over hedge is an excellent example. Here, an apple tree is trained as two horizontal branches only a short way above the ground. Growing the tree is not difficult – in essence it is training an apple tree as an espalier with just one horizontal tier – but it does require patience.

MATERIALS & EQUIPMENT

one 75 cm (30 in) metal or wooden post per 2 m (6 ft) length of hedge

galvanized wire • tensioning bolts

4 garden canes per tree

plant ties

spade • hammer

drill • secateurs

1 maiden whip apple tree per 4 m (12 ft) length of hedge

well-rotted organic material

1 planning the plot

Decide where you are going to put the trees and draw a plan to scale so that you can work out how many you will need and how much space they will take up. The distance between trees will vary depending on variety and stock, but they will usually extend at least 2 m (6 ft) on either side of the main stem when mature.

2 preparing the ground

Use pegs to mark out the planting sites on the ground and thoroughly prepare the ground in each position. Double-dig the ground, working in plenty of well-rotted organic material.

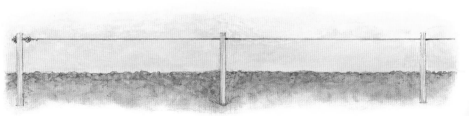

3 supporting the hedge

The apple hedge can usually support its own weight when mature. Before this, it must be held up by wires stretched taut between posts. Wooden posts are acceptable, as by the time they have rotted they are no longer needed. Metal posts can also be used, giving support even when the tree is mature. Whether wooden or metal, posts should be knocked into the ground at 2 m (6 ft) intervals; the wire stretched between them should be about 30 cm (12 in) from the ground.

4 stretching the wire

Use tensioning bolts to pull the horizontal wires tight. Twist the wire through the loop of the bolt and tighten the nut to tension.

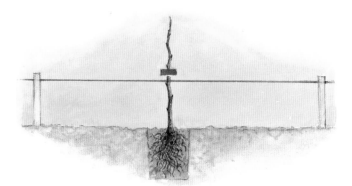

5 planting

Plant the young apple trees at their marked positions to the same depth as they were in their pots (or nursery beds if bare rooted). Cut off the leader just above the wire, ensuring that there are two buds roughly level with, or just below, the wire.

6 support for growing shoots

Tie two canes to the wire; angle them at about 45° using further canes to support their tops. As the two shoots grow, tie them to the canes. Remove any other shoots that may appear below.

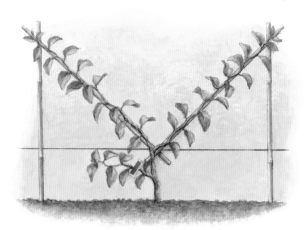

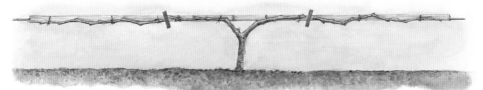

7 lowering the canes

In the winter of the first year, gently pull down the canes and tie them to the horizontal wires. Cut back both main shoots by about a third to a downward-facing bud. Any shoots that have grown off the main horizontals should be cut down to three or four buds.

8 summer pruning

Continue to prune as described above during the summer and winter of each year, allowing the horizontal shoots to grow longer until they have reached a length of about 2 m (6 ft). Cut back new side shoots to three or four buds and reduce new growth on existing side shoots to one leaf bud.

tall hedge
A higher apple hedge can be created by pruning several trees into multiple-stem cordons. Again, after a few years they will no longer require wire supports. Mature trees resemble a row of candelabras.

9 harvesting

The time for harvesting will depend on the variety used. As a rule of thumb, apples are usually ripe when they come away in the hand when gently twisted. On the whole, early varieties do not store, but later ones can be kept for several months in a cool place. Check periodically that none has rotted.

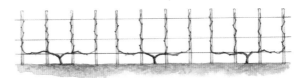

herb border

Herb gardens need a surprising amount of upkeep, and there are times of the
year – especially from late summer onwards – when they begin to look a bit tired.
One solution is to grow the herbs among other flowers in a mixed border. When in
season, the herbs add their fragrance and charm to the border; other plants take over
when the herbs are not at their best. Another benefit of a mixed planting is that herbs
can be harvested when ready without leaving conspicuous gaps in the garden.

MATERIALS & EQUIPMENT

10 x 1 cm (4 x ½ in) edging board
4 x 1 cm (1¾ x ½ in) pegs
stepping stones or broken slabs
2.4 m x 30 cm (8 x 1 ft) heavy-duty polythene sheet

spade • fork • rake • trowel
hammer • tamper

herbs and decorative plants in variety
well-rotted organic material

1   planning the border

Carefully draw out a plan of the permanent features of the
herb garden. Be sure to allow access to all parts of the plot
from a central gravel path by planning in stepping stones.
These can be square, circular or irregular paving slabs; they
do not need to be cemented in place and so can be moved
if the planting is changed. The plot shown here measures
2.4 m x 2.4 m (8 x 8 ft).

2   preparing the ground

Use pegs and string to mark out the position
of the path on the ground. Tamp down the soil
firmly, so that the gravel will be almost flush to
the ground when laid. Also tamp down the soil
where the stepping stones are to be laid.

3   making the path edging

To prevent the gravel spilling into the border,
construct a simple edging strip from lengths of
10 x 1 cm (4 x ½ in) treated timber. For every 90 cm
(3 ft) of edging board, nail in a 15 cm (6 in) upright
that has been sharpened to form a peg.

4   filling the path

Gently hammer the pegs (and edging board) into the ground along the
line of the path. Line the floor of the path with heavy-duty polythene
before pouring in the gravel – this will help suppress weed growth. Fill the
prepared path with a 10 cm (4 in) depth of gravel and rake the surface.

5   laying the stepping stones

When laying the paving slabs, bed them onto
a 5 cm (2 in) layer of sand to make them level.

6   preparing and planting

Dig over the bed in autumn, removing any perennial weeds and
adding well-rotted organic material. In spring, rake it through,
removing any new weeds that have appeared. Place the plants, still
in their pots, in position on the border. Stand back and try to
envisage them in full growth, making any necessary adjustments
to their positions. Mix the plants so that the herbs are scattered
throughout the border. This not only masks them during their less
interesting phases but also means that you can savour their
individual fragrances more easily. Plant out starting from the back
of the plot. Water well. Rake over the border to even the soil and
remove footprints. If you intend to mulch, do so now.

7 confining the mint

The mint and the white willowherb are both runners and are best confined to prevent them spreading over the other plants. Small areas can be controlled by planting in a bottomless bucket. Larger confined areas can be created by digging a trench around the planting and inserting a vertical layer of thick polythene, at least 30 cm (12 in) deep.

plant list
1 *Philadelphus* 'Sybille' x 1
2 *Foeniculum vulgare* (fennel) x 3
3 *Lathyrus odoratus* (sweet pea) x 8
4 *Angelica archangelica* (angelica) x 1
5 *Oenothera biennis* (evening primrose) x 3
6 *Cynara cardunculus* (cardoon) x 1
7 *Satureja montana* (winter savory) x 1
8 *Petroselinum crispum* (parsley) x 5
9 *Borago officinalis* (borage) x 3
10 *Epilobium angustifolium* 'Album' (willowherb) x 3
11 *Mentha spicata* (mint) x 3
12 *Aster* x *frikartii* x 1
13 *Lavandula stoechas pendunculata* x 1
14 *Nepeta* x *faasinnii* (catmint) x 2
15 *Allium tuberosum* (garlic chives) x 5
16 *Achillea millefolium* 'Cerise Queen' (yarrow) x 1
17 *Nepeta govaniana* x 3
18 *Lavandula angustifolia* (lavender) x 1
19 *Astrantia major* x 3
20 *Melissa officinalis* (lemon balm) x 1
21 *Laurus nobilis* (bay) x 2
22 *Thymus serpyllum* (thyme) x 3
23 *Nepeta sibirica* x 3
24 *Artemisia dracunculus* (French tarragon) x 3
25 *Origanum vulgare* (oregano) x 3
26 *Tanecetum parthenium* 'Aureum' x 2
27 *Ruta graveolens* (rue) x 1
28 *Calaminta grandiflora* (calamint) x 1
29 *Iris foetidissima* x 1
30 *Salvia officinalis* 'Icterina' (sage) x 1
31 *Levisticum officinalis* (lovage) x 1
32 *Anemone* x *hybrida* x 3
33 *Allium schoenoprasum* (chives) x 5
34 *Myrrhis odorata* (sweet Cicely) x 1
35 *Rosmarinus officinalis* (rosemary) x 1
36 *Pelargonium graveolens*
(scented geranium) x 3
37 *Geranium phaeum* x 1
38 *Dianthus* 'Miss Sinkins' x 3
39 *Alchemilla mollis* (lady's mantle) x 3
40 *Althaea officinalis* (marsh mallow) x 1

8 the complete plan

Draw up a complete planting plan. It is important not to underestimate the size to which some plants will grow. The plan is not sacrosanct and plants can change from year to year.

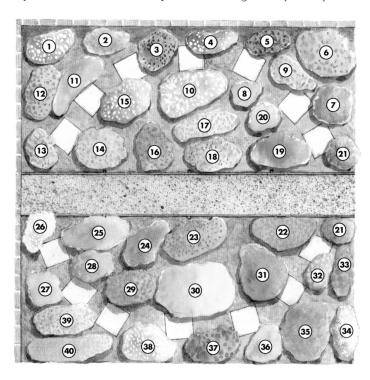

9 care and maintenance

Herb gardens tend to become scruffy if not given regular attention. Deadhead flowering stems unless seed is required and remove all vegetation that is dying back or already dead.

vegetables among the flowers

In many traditional cottage gardens, little differentiation was made between flowers, fruit and vegetables – the three were allowed to blend together organically or actually mixed when planting. Some vegetables can be as decorative as flowering plants and there is every reason to use them together when designing a garden. Mixing species in this way also offers some protection against the rapid proliferation of a particular pest or disease, which can occur in large stands of a single crop.

MATERIALS & EQUIPMENT

8 treated wooden posts 8 cm x 8 cm x 1.2 m (3 in x 3 in x 4 ft)

8 metal post supports to fit

stout galvanized wire

galvanized staples

sledge hammer • hammer

wire cutter • spade • fork

rake • secateurs

seed and plants in variety

well-rotted organic material

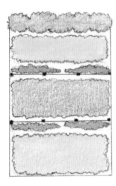

1 planning

Cottage gardens often seem randomly planted, but careful planning is called for to achieve this look. The garden contains permanent features, such as trees and fences, semi-permanent perennial flowering plants, as well as annuals and bedding plants. To help your planning, sketch out the plot using different blocks of colour for trees (blue), espalier trees (green), permanent planting (red), and vegetables and annuals (yellow).

2 fixing the posts

In this garden, two parallel fences support the espalier-trained pears and apples. Proprietary fences of metal uprights and thin metal cross-members are attractive but expensive; wire fences supported by four well-anchored wooden uprights will do the job just as well. Instead of digging holes for the wooden fence posts, use metal post supports. Drive them into the ground with a heavy sledge hammer. It helps to place an offcut of wood between post and hammer. Insert the wooden fence posts into the supports. Secure them by nailing through the holes at the base of the metal supports.

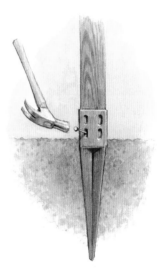

3 securing the cross wires

Stretch one length of galvanized wire horizontally across the faces of the four fence posts about 45 cm (18 in) above ground level. Secure with staples hammered into the wood. Strain the wire as tight as you can. Bend back the wire on the end posts and secure with a second staple to ensure that it does not work loose.

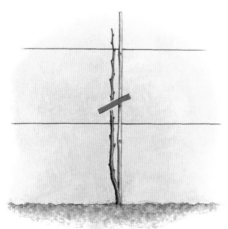

4 finishing the fence

Add a further two horizontal wires at 30 cm (12 in) intervals above the lowest wire. Erect a second fence of four posts parallel to the first. The posts should be treated with a wood preservative other than creosote.

5 espalier apples and pears

In early spring, plant two whip apple trees against one fence, and two whip pears against the other. Secure a cane vertically to the wires using plant ties. Use this to support the whip. After planting, cut the whip back to just above the lowest wire just above a bud that has two strong buds below.

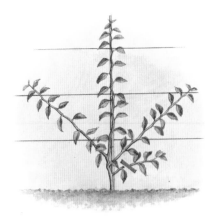

6 training

In summer, select two strong lateral shoots and secure them to canes tied in to the fence at 45° to the upright. Remove any other side shoots back to a couple of leaves; once the main first tier has become established these should be removed altogether, cutting them back flush to the trunk.

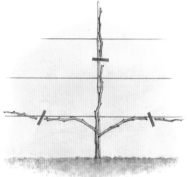

7 pruning

In the first winter, lower the lateral canes to a horizontal position to form the first tier of the espalier. Next, cut the vertical leader to just above the second wire – again, cut just above a bud that has two strong buds below. Repeat the steps above to form the next tiers of the espalier in the following two years.

plant list

1 *Helianthus annuus*
2 *Crocosmia* 'Lucifer' x 20
3 *Anthemis* 'Sauce Hollandaise' x 3
4 *Anthemis tinctoria* x 5
5 x *Solidaster luteus* x 2
6 *Hemerocallis* 'Stafford' x 3
7 *Kniphofia* 'Yellow Hammer' x 5

8 *apple bush trees in variety*
9 *whip apple trees for espaliers* x 2
10 *whip pears for espaliers* x 2
11 *leeks*
12 *parsnips*
13 *Swiss chard*
14 *spinach*

8 perennials

Plant the perennials in the prepared ground in spring at the same depth as they were in their pots. Do not plant them too close together because they will expand into clumps as they grow.

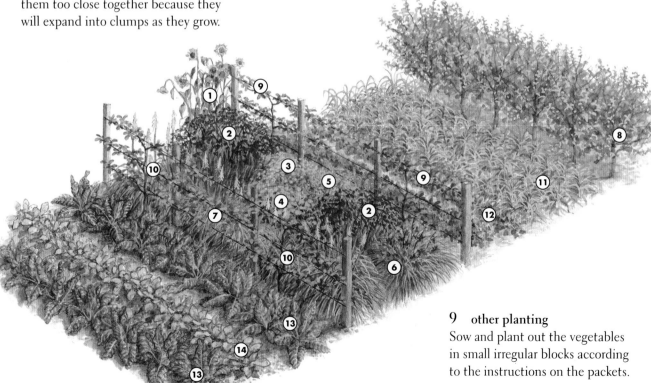

9 other planting

Sow and plant out the vegetables in small irregular blocks according to the instructions on the packets.

plant directory

A NOTE ON LATIN NAMES
Latin names are very rarely given on seed packets of fruit and vegetables; these are almost always sold by their common names. Herbs are usually referred to by their common names, though Latin names sometimes occur, while ornamentals are more frequently identified by their Latin names. Plants in this directory are listed according to these conventions.

VEGETABLES
Nearly all vegetables need an open, sunny position, away from overhanging foliage. In exposed areas, they should be protected from strong winds. The best soil for vegetables is a friable loam, either neutral or slightly acid, but they can be grown with success in most other types of soil except those of extreme acidity or alkalinity. Whatever the soil, it can usually be improved by the regular addition of organic material, such as compost or farmyard manure. Even the heaviest clay will eventually succumb.

Dig the soil over in the autumn so that it is open to the winter weather, which will help break it down to a fine tilth. Remove any weeds and add plenty of well-rotted organic material. When digging for the first time, it is best to double-dig – that is, to loosen the soil at the bottom of the trench that you are digging. However, avoid mixing this subsoil with the topsoil. Check for any weeds that have regenerated before planting in spring.

Do not sow or plant out too early. For hardy crops, wait until the soil has warmed up before sowing. Carrots, for example, will not germinate until the soil temperature is at least 7°C (45°F). Seed sown before this temperature is reached is liable to rot in the cold, damp soil. Tender crops, such as courgettes and many of the beans, should not be planted out or sown before all threat of frost has passed, or they could be killed.

Most vegetables can be sown directly where they are to grow, but it is sometimes more convenient or speedy to germinate them in pots or modules under glass and plant out when they are large enough. A few, such as celery, celeriac, and tomatoes, should always be started off under glass to ensure they grow fast enough to crop before the autumn. Do not plant too close together – allow room for the plant to develop. If planted too close, plants will become drawn and often sickly.

Keep crops weed-free and well watered. Mulch can be applied between plants to help keep weeds down and conserve moisture. Keep an eye out for pests and diseases and take appropriate action. A kitchen garden with healthy plants is less prone to attack than one in which the plants are neglected and weeds allowed to grow. Taller plants, such as beans and peas, may need support. Leafy ones such as lettuces and brassicas may need protection from birds, and most will need to be protected from slugs; wandering round the garden at night with a torch collecting slugs is enough to keep their populations in check.

Harvest vegetables as they ripen or as they are required for the table. Details for individual crops are given on the next pages. Some can be stored, while others, particularly root crops and some brassicas, such as Brussels sprouts, can be left in the ground as long as the weather does not get so cold that the ground freezes. If very cold weather threatens, lift the root vegetables and store them inside. In the listing, the term 'annual' refers to vegetables that complete their cycle within 12 months, although many are, in fact, biennials or tender perennials.

asparagus

Hardy perennial. Planted in spring at 30–38 cm (12–15 in) intervals in rows 90 cm (3 ft) apart. The 'spears' or shoots are harvested from late spring to early summer. Can be grown from seed sown in the spring. Harvest early summer. Best eaten fresh but can be frozen. Recommended variety: 'Lucullus'.

aubergine

Tender annual. Grown from seed sown in spring and kept in a greenhouse or planted outside in a warm position at 60 cm (24 in) intervals in rows 60 cm (24 in) apart once the frosts have passed. Good container plant. Harvest fruit when ripe. Best eaten fresh but can be kept a few days in a refrigerator.
Recommended varieties: 'Galine', 'Rima'.

beetroot

Hardy annual. Grown from seed sown where it is to grow in spring and thinned to 7.5–10 cm (3–4 in) intervals. Rows should be 30 cm (12 in) apart. Harvest when big enough. Best when eaten small. Can be left in the ground until required or stored in trays of just-moist sand in frost-free position.
Recommended varieties: 'Albina Vereduna' (white flesh), 'Boltardy', 'Burplees Golden' (yellow flesh), 'Monogram'.

broad bean

Hardy annual. Generally sown directly in the soil where it is to grow. Sow at 23 cm (9 in) intervals in rows set 30–90 cm (12–36 in) apart, depending on height of variety. Support taller varieties using cane pyramids or rows of canes. Harvest when the pods have swollen. Best eaten fresh but can be frozen.
Recommended varieties: 'Aquadulce', 'Imperial Green Longpod', 'Meteor', 'The Sutton'.

broccoli

Hardy annual. Grown from seed either sown in trays or *in situ*. Plant or thin to 60 cm (24 in) intervals in rows 60 cm (24 in) apart in early summer. Harvest leaves in spring. Best used fresh but can be frozen.
Recommended varieties: 'Minaret', 'Nine Star Perennial', 'Purple Sprouting'.

Brussels sprout

Hardy annual. Grown from seed sown in seed bed in spring and transplanted when big enough. Plant at 50–75 cm (20–30 in) intervals in rows 75 cm (30 in) apart. Harvest late autumn onwards. Can be left on plant until required. Best used fresh but can be frozen.
Recommended varieties: 'Bedford Fillbasket', 'Icarus', 'Peer Gynt', 'Rampart'.

cabbage

Hardy annual. Grown from seed sown in seed bed or under glass. Sow from spring to summer depending on variety. Plant at 50–75 cm (20–30 in) intervals in rows 75 cm (30 in) apart. Harvest throughout the year depending on variety. Pick as required.
Recommended varieties: 'Ruby Ball' (red cabbage), 'Ice Queen' (Savoy cabbage), 'First Early Market' (spring cabbage), 'Hispi', 'Duncan' (summer cabbages).

calabrese

Hardy annual. Can be sown in modules but best where they are to grow and thinned in late spring. Thin to or plant at 45 cm (18 in) intervals with the same distance between rows. Harvest autumn onwards. Best used fresh but can be frozen.
Recommended varieties: 'Mercedes', 'Shogun'.

carrot

Hardy annual. Sow very thinly where they are to grow from spring onwards. Thin to 8 cm (3 in) in rows set 20–25 cm (8–10 in) apart. Harvest when big enough. Can be left in ground until required or stored in trays of just-moist sand in a frost-free position.
Recommended varieties: 'Fly Away', 'Nanco'.

cauliflower

Hardy annual. Sow in seed bed in early spring for autumn varieties and early summer for winter varieties. Plant out at 50–75 cm (20–30 in) intervals in rows set 75 cm (30 in) apart. Harvest autumn onwards. Can be stored in a cool place for several weeks.
Recommended varieties: 'Aubade', 'Kestrel', 'White Rock'.

celeriac

Tender annual. Sow in trays under glass in spring. Plant out after frosts at 30 cm (12 in) intervals in rows set 40 cm (16 in) apart. Keep well watered. Harvest autumn onwards. Can be left in ground until required or stored in trays of just-moist sand in a frost-free position.
Recommended variety: 'Monarch'.

celery

Tender annual. Sow in trays under glass in spring. Plant out after frosts at 23–30 cm (9–12 in) intervals in rows set 30 cm (12 in) apart. Keep watered. Tie cardboard

collars round the stems and earth up to blanch. Harvest autumn onwards. Leave in the ground until required.
Recommended varieties: 'Giant Pink', 'Ivory Tower'.

chicory

Hardy biennial. Some are grown and used like lettuce; others (witloof) are forced to produce 'chicons', blanched shoots of tightly packed leaves. Sow in spring or early summer. Witloof is lifted in autumn; the roots are placed in pots of compost and covered with a light-proof pot. The chicons are harvested as required.
Recommended varieties: 'Witloof Zoom' (witloof), 'Red Treviso' (leaf chicory).

chilli

Tender annual. Sow in spring under glass and continue to grow under glass except in warm or sheltered areas. Plant 45–60 cm (18–24 in) apart if grown in the open, closer if in pots or growing bags. Harvest green or when ripe. Can be dried.
Recommended varieties: 'Apache', 'Hot Gold Spike'.

courgette

Tender annual; a small immature marrow. Sow in individual pots under glass. Plant out after frosts at 60 cm (24 in) intervals in rows 90 cm (36 in) apart. Harvest when small. Best eaten fresh but can be frozen.
Recommended varieties: 'Astoria', 'Early Gem', 'Supremo'.

cucumber

Tender annual. Sow in spring under glass. Either grow under glass climbing up strings, or as 'ridge' plants in the open, planting out after frosts at 60 cm (24 in) intervals in rows set 75 cm (30 in) apart. Harvest when large enough. Best fresh but can be stored for a few days.
Recommended varieties: 'Athene' (greenhouse), 'Bush Champion' (ridge).

endive

Hardy annual. Sow in late spring or summer *in situ* in rows set 35 cm (14 in) apart. Thin seedlings to 25 cm (10 in). Cover the centre of the plants with a plate or tile to blanch them. Harvest as required.
Recommended varieties: 'Pancaliere', 'Full Heart Italian'.

fennel

Hardy perennial. Sow direct where it is to grow or under glass from early summer onwards. Thin to or plant at 30 cm (12 in) intervals in rows set 60 cm (24 in) apart. As bulbs swell, earth up around to blanch the leaves. Harvest when big enough for the table. Best eaten fresh, but can be frozen.
Recommended varieties: 'Cantino', 'Sweet Florence'.

French bean

Tender annual. Sow direct where it is to grow from late spring onwards. Thin to 10 cm (4 in) intervals in rows set 45 cm (18 in) apart. Harvest from summer onwards. Climbing varieties can be grown as runner beans. Best used fresh but can be frozen.
Recommended varieties: 'Annabel', 'Vilbel'.

garlic

Hardy annual. Plant the bulbs in late autumn or spring at 15 cm (6 in) intervals in rows set 25 cm (10 in) apart. Harvest and dry in midsummer. Dry after lifting and store in a cool frost-free place.
Recommended varieties: usually sold simply as garlic.

rooftop kitchen garden

potager

globe artichoke
Hardy perennial. Plant in spring at 75 cm (30 in) intervals in rows set 1.2 m (4 ft) apart. Harvest flower buds in summer before they open. Best eaten fresh, although 'hearts' can be frozen.
Recommended variety: 'Vert de Laon'.

Jerusalem artichoke
Hardy annual. Plant the tubers 15 in (6 in) deep at 30 cm (12 in) intervals in rows 120 cm (4 ft) apart. Harvest from autumn onwards. Leave in ground until required or lift and store in a cool, dark place.
Recommended variety: 'Fuseau'.

kale
Hardy annual. Sow in seed bed or in trays in spring. Plant out in rows set 60 cm (24 in) apart at 45 cm (18 in) intervals. Harvest from late autumn onwards. Eat fresh.
Recommended varieties: 'Bornick', 'Fribor'.

kohl rabi
Hardy annual. Sow directly where it is to grow from spring onwards in rows set 30 cm (12 in) apart. Thin seedlings to 20 cm (8 in) intervals. Harvest when large enough. Eat as required, preferably while still quite small.
Recommended varieties: 'Green Vienna', 'Purple Vienna', 'Rowel'.

leek
Hardy annual. Sow in spring in seed bed or in trays/modules. Plant out in rows 30 cm (12 in) apart at 15 cm (6 in) intervals. Harvest when large enough. Leave in the ground until required.
Recommended varieties: 'Autumn Mammoth-Goliath', 'Cortina'.

lettuce
Tender/hardy annual. Sow directly where it is to grow or in trays under glass from spring onwards. Thin to or plant out at 23 cm (9 in) intervals in rows set 30 cm (12 in) apart. Harvest when large enough. Lift whole plant as required. For cut-and-come-again varieties, harvest individual leaves as required.
Recommended varieties: 'Bubble', 'Little Gem', 'Lollo Rossa', 'Winter Density'.

marrow
Tender annual. Sow under glass in late spring or *in situ* after frosts have passed. Plant out (or sow) 90 cm (3 ft) apart for bush varieties and 150 cm (5 ft) apart for trailing varieties. Harvest when large enough. Can be stored for a few weeks in a frost-free place if hardened off in the sun first.
Recommended varieties: 'All Green Bush', 'Long Green Trailing'.

onion
Hardy bulb. Can be grown from seed or 'sets' (small bulbs). Plant sets in spring at 10 cm (4 in) intervals in rows set 30 cm (12 in) apart. Sow seed in winter under glass and plant out seedlings at intervals as above. Harvest in summer when the leaves begin to yellow. Dry in the sun and then store in a cool, frost-free place.
Recommended varieties: 'Giant Fen Globe', 'Sturon'.

parsnip
Hardy annual. Sow where it is to grow in early spring in rows set 30 cm (12 in) apart. Thin seedlings to 15–20 cm (6–8 in) apart. Harvest from late autumn onwards. Leave in the ground until required.
Recommended varieties: 'Javelin', 'Tender and True'.

pea
Tender annual. Sow in double rows from spring onwards at 5 cm (2 in) intervals. Rows should be 60–80 cm (2–3 ft) apart depending on variety. Support taller varieties with sticks or netting. Harvest once pods swell. Best eaten fresh but can be frozen.
Recommended varieties: 'Early Onward', 'Hurst Greenshaft', 'Oregon Sugar Pod'.

pepper
Tender annual. Sow in spring under glass and continue to grow under glass except in warm or sheltered areas. Plant 45–60 cm (18–24 in) apart in the open, closer in pots or growing bags. Harvest green or when ripe. Best eaten fresh but can be kept for a week or so in cool conditions.
Recommended varieties: 'Ace', 'Carnival', 'Gold Star'.

potato
Tender annual. Plant seed tubers 30–38 cm (12–15 in) apart in a trench 15 cm (6 in) deep from early spring onwards. Adjacent rows should be 75 cm (30 in) apart. Draw up the soil around the growing stems and protect from frost. Harvest from summer onwards.
Recommended varieties: 'Foremost' (early), 'Estima' (second early), 'Cara' (maincrop), 'Pink Fir Apple' (salad).

pumpkin

Tender annual. Sow seed under glass in spring and plant out after frosts have passed at 90–180 cm (3–6 ft) intervals, depending on variety. Harvest when large enough and before frosts. Some varieties can be hardened off in the sun and then stored in a cool place for several months.
Recommended varieties: 'Atlantic Giant' (for size), 'Crown Prince' (for flavour).

radish

Tender/hardy annual. Sow *in situ* from spring onwards in rows set 15 cm (6 in) apart. Thin seedlings to 2.5–5 cm (1–2 in) apart. Harvest when large enough, as required.
Recommended varieties: 'French Breakfast', 'Prinz Rotin', 'Sparkler'.

rhubarb

Hardy perennial. Plant 'crowns' in winter at 75–90 cm (30–36 in) intervals. Early crops can be raised each year by forcing – covering the plants with a special pot or a bucket. Harvest the stalks from spring onwards. Best fresh, but can be frozen or bottled.
Recommended varieties: 'Champagne', 'Timperly Early'.

runner bean

Tender annual. Sow *in situ* or in individual pots under glass from late spring onwards. Plant out after frosts. Thin or plant at 25–30 cm (10–12 in) intervals with rows set 90–120 cm (3–4 ft) apart. Support the beans on poles, or netting. Harvest from midsummer onwards. Best used fresh but can be frozen.
Recommended varieties: 'Enorma', 'Liberty'.

salsify

Hardy annual. Sow where it is to grow in spring in rows set 25 cm (10 in) apart. Thin the seedlings to 15 cm (6 in) intervals. Harvest from late autumn onwards. Can be left in ground until required or stored in trays of just-moist sand in a frost-free position.

seakale

Hardy perennial. Plant crowns in spring 5 cm (2 in) deep, 38 cm (15 cm) apart, in rows set 45 cm (18 in) apart. Cover the plant in midwinter with a light-proof pot.

Harvest blanched stalks in early spring; eat as it matures.
Recommended varieties: usually sold simply as seakale.

shallot

Hardy bulb. Plant the bulbs just below the surface at 15 cm (6 in) intervals with 30 cm (12 in) between rows. Harvest in summer. Dry off in the sun and then store in a cool, frost-free place.
Recommended varieties: 'Dutch Yellow', 'Hative de Niort', 'Sante'.

spinach

Tender/hardy perennial. Sow where it is to grow in spring onwards in rows set 30 cm (12 in) apart. Thin the seedlings to 15 cm (6 in). Harvest when leaves large enough. Best used fresh but can be frozen.
Recommended varieties: 'Monnopa', 'Sigmaleaf'.

spring onion

Hardy annual. Sow *in situ* in rows set 15–20 cm (6–8 in) apart. Thin if necessary to 2.5 cm (1 in) apart. Harvest when big enough. Pull and eat as required.
Recommended varieties: 'White Lisbon', 'Winter Over'.

swede

Hardy annual. Sow *in situ* in early summer in rows set 45 cm (18 in) apart. Thin seedlings to 30 cm (12 in) intervals. Harvest from late autumn onwards. Can be left in ground until required or stored in trays of just-moist sand in a frost-free position.
Recommended varieties: 'Best of All', 'Marian'.

sweetcorn

Tender annual. Sow under glass in spring and plant out when frosts have passed. Plant in a block at 30 cm (12 in) intervals each way. Harvest after tassels have withered and cob is plump. Best used fresh but can be frozen.
Recommended varieties: 'Sundance', 'Kelvedon Glory'.

Swiss chard

Hardy annual. Sow in spring where it is to grow in rows set 45 cm (18 in) apart. Thin seedlings to 30 cm (12 in) intervals. Harvest when leaves large enough. Cut leaves as required, cover with cloches in colder areas.
Recommended varieties: 'Foordhook Giant', 'Lucullus', 'Rhubarb Chard'.

tomato

Tender annual. Grow from seed under glass in spring and either continue under glass in pots or grow-bags, or plant out after frosts have passed. Plant at 60 cm (24 in) intervals. Cordon varieties need support and should have any side shoots removed. Bush varieties need neither. Pick when ripe. Can be frozen, bottled or dried.
Recommended varieties: 'Dombito', 'Gardener's Delight (cherry), 'Tigerella', 'Ida Gold' (bush), 'Totem' (bush).

turnip

Hardy annual. Sow in spring where they are to grow in rows set 30 cm (12 in) apart. Thin to 15 cm (6 in) intervals. Harvest when large enough. Can be left in ground until required or stored in trays of just-moist sand in a frost-free position.
Recommended varieties: 'Golden Ball', 'Purple Top Milan', 'Snowball'.

FRUIT

Most fruit needs a sunny position that is open yet protected from strong winds. The soil should be well prepared because the plants are likely to stay in the same place for many years. Remove all weeds and add plenty of well-rotted organic material, such as compost or farmyard manure. Plant any time between mid-autumn and early spring, as long as the weather is neither too wet nor too cold. Cane fruit and many trained tree fruits need support.

Keep the soil at the base of trees and bushes weed-free, but avoid hoeing too deep and disturbing the roots. Top-dress the soil in autumn and spring with well-rotted organic material. Protect ripening fruit from bird attack by enclosing the plants in a fruit cage or loose netting. In some areas it will also be necessary to protect emerging buds from birds, but it is usually better to allow birds access outside the fruiting season because they will remove insect pests. If insects are a continuous problem, they should be dealt with using organic or chemical means: seek advice from a garden centre or nursery.

Most fruit needs to be harvested once it has fully ripened, although fruit for storing is often best picked slightly before it ripens. Apples, pears and quinces are the only fruit generally stored in the natural state. Other fruit may be frozen or bottled.

apple

Can be grown as trees, bushes, cordons, dwarf pyramids, espaliers, fans or poles. Harvest in autumn. Many varieties can be stored in cool, frost-free conditions.

apricot

Can be grown as bush trees or fans, preferably against a wall. Harvest in early autumn. Best eaten fresh, but can be dried or bottled.

blackberry

Grown on canes supported on wires. Harvest from late summer onwards. Best eaten fresh, but they can be frozen or bottled.

blackcurrant

Grown as bushes. Harvest in summer. Best used fresh but can be frozen or bottled.

blueberry

Grown as bushes. Harvest in summer onwards. Best used fresh but can be frozen or bottled.

Calamondin orange

strawberry

cherry
Can be grown as trees, bush trees or fans. Harvest in midsummer. Best used fresh but can be frozen or bottled.

damson
Can be grown as trees, bush trees and fans. Harvest from autumn onwards. Best used fresh but can be frozen or bottled.

fig
Can be grown as trees, bush trees or fans, preferably against a wall. Harvest in autumn. Best eaten fresh but can be dried.

gooseberry
Grown as bushes, cordons or standards. Harvest in summer. Best used fresh but can be frozen or bottled.

grape
Grown as a vine on supports or against a wall. Harvest in autumn. Best eaten fresh, but can be turned into wine.

loganberry
Grown as canes against wire supports. Harvest in late summer. Best used fresh but can be frozen or bottled.

mulberry
Grown as a tree. Harvest in late summer or early autumn. Best used fresh but can be frozen or bottled.

nectarine
Grown as bush trees or fans, preferably against walls. Harvest early autumn. Best eaten fresh.

peach
Grown as a bush, tree or fan, preferably against a wall. Harvest early autumn. Best eaten fresh.

pear
Can be grown as trees, bushes, cordons, dwarf pyramids, espaliers, fans or poles. Harvest in autumn. Best eaten fresh but can be stored in a cool place.

plum
Grown as trees, bush trees and fans. Harvest late summer onwards. Best used fresh but can be frozen or bottled.

quince
Grown as trees, preferably in moist soil. Harvest late autumn. Can be stored in a cool place for several months. Store apart from other fruit as its fragrance pervades all.

raspberry
Grown as canes against wire supports. Harvest from early summer onwards. Best very fresh; can be frozen or bottled.

redcurrant
Grown as bushes, cordons, fans or standards. Harvest in summer. Best used fresh but can be frozen or bottled.

strawberry
Grown as hardy perennials in the ground or in containers. Harvest from early summer onwards. Best used fresh but can be frozen or bottled.

whitecurrant
Grown as bushes, cordons, fans or standards. Harvest in summer. Best used fresh but can be frozen or bottled.

pear

redcurrant

CULINARY HERBS

Herbs can be grown in a dedicated herb garden, in the vegetable plot, mixed in with ornamental plants in decorative borders, or in pots. They generally like a free-draining soil that is not too rich. Thoroughly prepare the ground in autumn ready for spring planting. Remove all weeds and add organic material to improve the soil's structure but do not add any extra fertilizer; there will be enough feed in the humus.

Plant in spring, watering thoroughly. Allow plenty of space for shrubby plants, such as the sages, to spread. Some herbs, including mint, are notorious spreaders and must be contained in some way to prevent them invading other plants. Herb gardens should have paths or stepping stones included in their design for easy access.

Best quality herbs are obtained by picking the leaves when still young, preferably before the plants flower. After this, the leaves may still be usable on some plants, such as thyme, but on others they become tired and tough. Once herbaceous plants have flowered, they tend to look bedraggled and should be cut back. Annuals can be removed. However, if you want the seeds, leave a few old flowering stems until the seed has ripened. Do not eat or cook with seed that has been sold for sowing, because this may have been chemically treated.

Hang bunches of stems to dry in a warm, airy place out of direct sunlight. Drying in an oven is too quick. Hang bunches of seed heads in muslin bags in a warm, airy place. When leaves and seed are completely dry, store them in airtight, light-proof containers. Herbs can be frozen in plastic freezer bags, or as ice cubes in small quantities. Chop the leaves and add them to water in an ice cube tray. The cube can later be used in a dish.

In the list below, only the most 'usual' reason, or reasons, for growing a herb are given: many can also be grown for other parts of the plant that have decorative, medicinal or other value.

angelica (*Angelica archangelica*)
Biennial or longer. 1–2.5 m (3–8 ft) high. Grown for stem, seed and leaves. Sow in autumn or spring in a pot or *in situ*. Plant at or thin to 90 cm (3 ft) intervals. Harvest stems in summer, seed in late summer/autumn, leaves before flowering. Leaves can be dried and stems candied.

anise (*Pimpinella anisum*)
Annual. 30–45 cm (12–18 in) high. Grown for its seed and leaves. Sow *in situ* in spring. Thin to 20 cm (8 in). Harvest as required. The seeds can be dried and stored.

basil (*Ocimum basilicum*)
Tender annual. 45 cm (18 in) high. Grown for its leaves. Sow under glass or after frosts *in situ*. Plant at or thin to 20 cm (8 in) intervals. Harvest leaves as required. The leaves can be dried for storage.

bay (*Laurus nobilis*)
Hardy evergreen shrub. Up to 4.5 m (15 ft) high. Grown for its leaves. Buy as a container plant or take cuttings in late summer and plant out resulting plants when big enough. Can be topiaried. Harvest leaves as required. Dried leaves are sweeter than fresh ones.

bergamot (*Monarda didyma*)
Hardy perennial. 90 cm (3 ft) high. Grown for its leaves. Buy as a container plant or divide an existing plant in spring. Plant at 60 cm (2 ft) intervals. Harvest leaves as required. The leaves can be dried for storage.

borage (*Borago officinalis*)
Annual. 75 cm (30 in) high. Grown for its flowers and young leaves. Sow seeds in a pot or *in situ*. Thin to or plant out at 30 cm (12 in) intervals. Harvest leaves young and flowers when required. Flowers can be frozen in ice cubes or crystallized.

caraway (*Carum carvi*)
Annual or biennial. 60 cm (2 ft) high. Grown for its seed and leaves. Sow seed *in situ* in autumn. Thin seedlings in spring to 20 cm (8 in) intervals. Harvest leaves when young and seed in late summer when ripe. The seeds can be dried for storage.

chamomile (*Chamaemelum nobile*)
Hardy perennial. 25 cm (10 in) high. Grown for its leaves. Sow in spring in pots, or divide an existing plant, and plant out at 15 cm (6 in) intervals. Harvest leaves at any time. The leaves can be dried for storage.

chervil (*Anthriscus cerefolium*)
Annual. 38 cm (15 in) high. Grown for its leaves. Sow *in situ* from spring onwards for a continuous supply. Thin to 20 cm (8 in). Harvest leaves before flowering.

chives (*Allium schoenoprasum*)
Perennial bulb. 30 cm (12 in) high. Grown for its leaves. Buy a container plant or divide an existing one in spring. Plant out 20 cm (8 in) apart. Harvest as required. The leaves can be dried or frozen for storage.

coriander (*Coriander sativum*)
Biennial. 60 cm (2 ft) high. Grown for its leaves and seeds. Sow in autumn or spring *in situ* and thin to 20 cm (8 in) intervals. Harvest leaves as required and seeds when ripe. Dry seeds and freeze leaves for storage.

dill (*Anethum graveolens*)
Annual. Up to 1.5 m (5 ft) high. Grown for its leaves and seed. Sow *in situ* from spring onwards. Thin to 25 cm (10 in) intervals. Harvest leaves when young and seed when ripe. Dry leaves and seeds for storage.

fennel (*Foeniculum vulgare*)
Hardy perennial. 2.2 m (7 ft) high. Grown for its leaves and seed. Sow in spring in pots or *in situ*. Thin or plant out to 60 cm (24 in) intervals. Harvest leaves as required, seed when ripe. Dry seeds and freeze leaves for storage.

horseradish (*Armoracia rusticana*)
Hardy perennial. 60 cm (2 ft) high. Grown for its roots. Plant or divide an existing plant in spring. Plant at 45 cm (18 in) intervals. Leave in the ground until needed: in very cold areas, lift a few roots and store in just-moist sand in a frost-free place over winter.

hyssop (*Hyssopus officinalis*)
Hardy shrub. 60 cm (2 ft) high. Grown for its leaves. Buy as a container plant or take cuttings from an existing plant in summer. Plant at 60 cm (2 ft) intervals. Harvest leaves as required; they can be dried for storage.

lemon balm (*Melissa officinalis*)
Hardy perennial. 90 cm (3 ft) high. Grown for its leaves. Buy a container plant or divide an existing plant in spring. Plant out at 60 cm (2 ft) intervals. Harvest leaves as required. The leaves can be dried for storage.

lovage (*Levisticum officinale*)
Hardy perennial. 2.2 m (7 ft) high. Grown for its leaves and seed. Buy a plant or sow seed in autumn. Plant out at 75 cm (30 in) intervals. Harvest leaves as needed and seed when ripe. Dry or freeze leaves for storage.

marjoram (*Origanum marjorana*)
Annual or tender perennial. 60 cm (24 in) high. Grown for its leaves. Grow from seed in spring. Plant out at 45 cm (18 in) intervals. Harvest as required. The leaves can be dried or frozen for storage.

mint (*Mentha spp.*)
Hardy perennial. 60 cm (24 in) high. Grown for its leaves. Buy a container plant or divide an existing plant. Plant at 30 cm (12 in) intervals. Rampant spreaders, so best contained. Harvest leaves as required and dry or freeze for storage.

mustard (*Brassica spp.*)
Annual. Up to 1.8 m (6 ft) high. Grown for its seed and young leaves. Sow in spring, thinning to 15 cm (6 in). Harvest salad leaves a few days after sowing and seeds as they ripen in late summer. Dry seed for storage.

oregano (*Origanum vulgare*)
Hardy perennial. 60 cm (24 in) high. Grown for its leaves. Grow from seed or by division of an existing plant in spring. Plant out at 45 cm (18 in) intervals. Harvest as required. Leaves can be dried or frozen for storage.

parsley (*Petroselinum crispum*)
Biennial. 30 cm (12 in) high. Grown for its leaves. Sow in spring *in situ* or in pots. Thin to or plant out at 23 cm (9 in) intervals. Harvest leaves as required and dry or freeze for storage.

rosemary (*Rosmarinus officinalis*)
Hardy evergreen shrub. Up to 1.8 m (6 ft) high. Grown for its leaves. Buy a container plant or take cuttings in summer. Plant out in spring at 1.5 m (5 ft) intervals. Harvest leaves as required. The leaves can be dried.

sage (*Salvia officinalis*)
Hardy evergreen shrub. 75 cm (30 in) high. Grown for its leaves. Buy a container plant or take cuttings in summer. Plant out in spring at 1 m (3 ft) intervals. Harvest the leaves as required. The leaves can be dried for storage.

savory, summer (*Satureja hortensis*)
Annual. 45 cm (18 in) high. Grown for its leaves. Sow in spring in pots or *in situ*. Plant out or thin to 23 cm (9 in) intervals. Harvest leaves as required and dry for storage.

savory, winter (*Satureja montana*)
Hardy shrub. 45 cm (18 in) high. Grown for its leaves. Buy as a container plant or take

cuttings from an existing plant in summer. Plant out at 45 cm (18 in) intervals. Harvest the leaves as required and dry for storage.

sweet Cicely (*Myrrhis odorata*)
Hardy perennial. 75 cm (30 in) high. Grown for seeds and leaves. Sow in autumn or spring either in pots or *in situ*. Plant out or thin to 60 cm (24 in) intervals. Harvest leaves while young and seed either while they are still green or when they are fully ripe. Dry unripe seed for storage.

tarragon (*Artemisia dracunculus*)
Tender/hardy perennial. 60 cm (24 in) high. Grown for its leaves. Buy container plants or take cuttings in summer. Plant at 45 cm (18 in) intervals. Harvest leaves as required. The leaves can be dried or frozen for storage.

thyme (*Thymus spp.*)
Hardy shrub. Up to 30 cm (12 in) high. Grown for its leaves. Buy as a container plant or take cuttings from an existing plant in summer. Plant out at 30 cm (12 in) intervals. Harvest leaves as required. The leaves can be dried for storage.

DECORATIVE AND OTHER EDIBLE PLANTS
A kitchen garden commonly contains plants other than crops. Some are chosen for their decorative value and are mixed in with the food plants to add visual interest throughout the year; others are grown because they attract beneficial insects to the garden; and still other species, which are not considered to be food plants, have edible flowers and are worth growing for use in salads or just as a garnish. The following list gives details of just a few such plants.

Allium schoenoprasum (chives)
Perennial bulb. 30 cm (12 in) high. Grown in the herb garden for its leaves, but also has attractive, edible purple flowers.

Allium tuberosum (Chinese chives)
Perennial bulb. Up to 45 cm (18 in) high. Grown in the herb garden for its leaves, but also has attractive, edible white flowers. It makes a perfect plant for edging beds. Remove flower stalks after flowering.

Althea rosea (hollyhock)
Short-lived perennial/hardy annual. Up to 2.2 m (7 ft) high. Grown in old-fashioned cottage gardens for its towering flower spikes. The flowers are edible. Remove after flowering if it is suffering from rust.

Amaranthus giganticus (leafy amaranth)
Tender annual. Up to 60 cm (2 ft) high. Exotic plant with colourful tassels of flowers. The leaves are edible. Sow *in situ* after the frosts have finished or start under glass.

Amaranthus hypochondriacus (grain amaranth)
Tender annual. Up to 3 m (10 ft) high. Towering plant with shaggy tassels of colourful flowers. Grown for its decorative qualities and edible seeds. Sow *in situ* after frosts have passed or start under glass.

Atriplex hortensis (red orache)
Hardy annual. Up to 1.8 m (6 ft) high. A tall, decorative plant with red stems and foliage. The young leaves can be eaten like spinach. Will self-sow if left to seed.

Bellis perennis (English daisy)
Perennial/hardy biennial. Up to 15 cm (6 in) high. A low plant with white, pink or red edible flowers, ideal for edging beds. Sow *in situ* or in trays. Plant out in spring.

Borago officinalis (borage)
Annual. 75 cm (30 in) high. A herb grown for its flowers and young leaves. It has a lax habit and flops over other plants but it is valuable in the decorative garden for its grey foliage and blue flowers. Sow seeds in a pot or where it is to grow. Will self-sow.

Buxus sempervirens (box)
Shrub. Very useful for low hedging. Plant at 20 cm (8 in) intervals; trim as they reach the shape of the required hedge. Also good for topiaried accent plants, either in the ground or in containers.

Calendula officinalis (pot marigold)
Hardy annual. Up to 45 cm (18 in) high. Grown in the herb garden for its leaves and bright orange flowers. Sow *in situ* in autumn or spring. If left it will self-sow.

Chenopodium bonus-henricus (Good King Henry)
Perennial. Up to 45 cm (18 in) high. A leafy plant that looks like a weed but is grown for its young leaves, eaten like spinach in spring. Grow from seed or by division.

Chenopodium giganteum (tree spinach)
Hardy annual. Up to 2.5 m (8 ft) high. Very fast growing, tall plant with green leaves that take on a reddish tinge. The leaves can be eaten like spinach. Sow where it is to grow. It is likely to self-sow prodigiously.

Curcubita spp. (ornamental gourd)
Tender annual. Up to 1.8 cm (6 ft) high. Ornamental varieties of squashes and pumpkins cannot be eaten but make very decorative climbing or trailing plants. Start under glass and plant out after frosts.

Fragaria vesca (alpine strawberry)
Hardy perennial. Up to 25 cm (10 in) high. Strawberry plants with delicious miniature fruit that flower and fruit over a very long period and make ideal plants for edging a bed. Grown from divisions or seed.

Helianthus annuus (sunflower)
Hardy annual. Up to 3 m (10 ft) high. Tall decorative plants grown for their flowers and edible seed and petals. Sow *in situ* or in pots.

Hemerocallis spp. (day lily)
Hardy perennial. Up to 1.2 m (4 ft) high. Day lilies are attractive but take up quite a lot of space. The flowers are colourful and good to eat in salads or stir-fried while they are still in bud. Plant out divisions in spring.

Humulus lupulus aureus (golden hop)
Hardy perennial. Up to 4.5 m (15 ft) high. Rapid climbers perfect for covering posts or trellises. The young shoots are a delicacy when cooked like asparagus and the female flowers (hops) can be used for beer-making. Plant out divisions in spring.

Laurus nobilis (sweet bay)
Hardy evergreen shrub. Up to 4.5 m (15 ft) high. Grown as a herb for its leaves. Highly decorative when cut into a ball or other topiary shape. Grow from seed or cuttings.

Lavandula angustifolia (lavender)
Hardy shrub. Up to 60 cm (2 ft) high. Grown for its appearance and scent; the flowers can be used to flavour and perfume food. Grow from cuttings.

Malus sylvestris (crab apple)
Hardy tree. Up to 6 m (20 ft) high. Decorative blossom in spring that is useful as a pollinator for other apple trees. The small fruit are useful for making preserves.

Papaver somniferum (opium poppy)
Hardy annual. Up to 1.2 m (4 ft) high. A decorative plant of no culinary value. A slender plant with pink, purple, red or white flowers that self-sow.

Rosa (rose)
Climber or shrub. Up to 6 m (20 ft) high. Decorative plants useful for growing over arches and up through old trees. The hips of wild varieties can be used for syrup and the flowers are edible.

Tagetes erecta (marigold)
Tender annual. Up to 30 cm (12 in) high. A colourful (gold and mahogany) addition to the vegetable garden, but also grown to deter whitefly and other pests. Grow from seed under glass; plant out after frosts have passed.

Tropaeolum majus (nasturtium)
Tender annual. Up to 60 cm (2 ft) high. A colourful climber and trailer that can be used to cover bare ground. Its flowers can be used in salads. Grow seed under glass and plant out after frosts have passed.

Viola odorata (sweet violet)
Hardy perennial. Up to 15 cm (6 in) high. Grown for its violet, purple or white flowers that can be used as a table decoration or the petals added to sweets. It can be crystallized. Plant out from divisions or seed.

Viola tricolor (heartsease)
Hardy perennial. Up to 15 cm (6 in) high. Miniature pansies that have a habit of self-sowing around the vegetable garden. The petals are edible. Grow from seed.

Viola x wittrockiana (pansy)
Hardy perennial. Up to 15 cm (6 in) high. Valuable as an edging or decorative plant, especially in the winter when there is not much else about. The petals are edible. Grow from seed or cuttings.

herb border

useful addresses

**GENERAL VEGETABLE
SEED SUPPLIERS**
*Available at garden centres
and by mail order from:*

Chiltern Seeds
Bortree Stile
Ulverston
Cumbria LA12 7PB
01229 581137
www.chilternseeds.co.uk

DT Brown and Co.
Bury Road
Newmarket
Suffolk CB8 7PR
0845 1662275
www.dtbrownseeds.co.uk

Johnsons Seeds
Gazeley Road
Kentford
Newmarket
Suffolk CB8 7QB
01638 554123
www.johnsons-seeds.com

Marshalls
Regal Road, Wisbech
Cambridgeshire PE13 2RF
01945 583407
www.marshalls-seeds.co.uk

Mr Fothergill's Seeds
Gazeley Road
Kentford
Newmarket
Suffolk CB8 7QB
01638 751161
www.mr-fothergills.co.uk

Samuel Dobie
Long Road
Paignton
Devon TQ4 7SX
0870 1123623
www.dobies.co.uk

Suttons Seeds Ltd
Woodview Road
Paignton
Devon TQ4 7NG
0870 2202899
www.suttons-seeds.co.uk

Thompson & Morgan
Poplar Lane
Ipswich
Suffolk IP8 3BU
01473 588821
www.thompson-morgan.com

Unwins Seed Ltd
Telephone 01244 882555
for your nearest stockist.
www.unwins-seeds.co.uk

**MORE UNUSUAL
VEGETABLE SEED**

**Association Kokopelli
Organic Seeds**
www.terredesemences.com

Chase Organics
Riverdene Business Park
Molesey Road
Hersham
Surrey KT12 4RG
01932 253666
www.chaseorganics.co.uk

Edwin Tucker
Brewery Meadow
Stonepark
Ashburton
Devon TQ13 7DG
01364 652233
www.edwintucker.com

Future Foods
Luckleigh Cottage
Hockworthy
Wellington
Somerset TA21 0NN
01398 361347
www.futurefoods.com

Heritage Seed Library
(members only)
Henry Doubleday Research
Association
Ryton Organic Gardens
Coventry
Warwickshire CV8 3LG
024 7630 3517
www.hdra.org.uk

Kings
Monk's Farm
Kelvedon, Colchester
Essex CO5 9PG
01376 570000
www.kingsseeds.com

Seeds-by-Size
45 Crouchfield
Boxmoor
Hemel Hempstead
Hertfordshire HP1 1PA
01442 251458
www.seeds-by-size.co.uk

Suffolk Herbs
Monk's Farm
Kelvedon
Colchester
Essex CO5 9PG
01376 572456
www.suffolkherbs.com

Thomas Etty
45 Forde Avenue
Bromley
Kent BR1 3EU
020 8466 6785

**FENCING, HURDLES
AND GATES**

British Gates & Timber
Castletons Oak
Sawmills
Biddenden
Kent TN27 8DD
01580 291555
www.britishgates.co.uk

English Hurdle
Curload
Stoke St. Gregory
Taunton
Somerset TA3 6JD
01823 698418
www.englishhurdle.co.uk

Forest Fencing
Stanford Court
Stanford Bridge
nr Worcester
Worcestershire WR6 6SR
01886 812451

Stuart Garden Architecture
Burrow Hill Farm
Wiveliscombe
Somerset TA4 2RN
01984 667458
www.stuartgarden.com

TRELLIS
*Available from most garden
centres and the following:*

**Anthony de Grey Gardens
and Trellises**
Broadhinton Yard
77a North Street
London SW4 0HQ
020 7738 8866
www.anthonydegrey.com

Frolics of Winchester
The Workshop
Vale Farm Pitt
Winchester
Hampshire SO22 5QW
01962 869219

Trelysian Ltd
31 Collwood Close
Poole
Dorset BH15 3HG
01202 385181

BUILDING SUPPLIES
*Many garden centres stock
some building materials. Also
try local building centres.
General suppliers include:*

B & Q plc
Telephone 0845 3093099
for your nearest branch.
www.diy.com

Focus
www.focusdiy.co.uk

Homebase
Telephone 0845 0778888
for your nearest branch.
www.homebase.co.uk

Wickes
Telephone 0870 6089001
for your nearest branch.
www.wickes.co.uk

SOCIETIES

**Henry Doubleday Research
Association**
Details as above.

National Vegetable Society
0161 4427190
www.nvsuk.org.uk

**Royal Horticultural
Society**
80 Vincent Square
London SW1P 2PE
020 7834 4333
www.rhs.org.uk

credits

The publishers would like to thank the following garden owners and designers for allowing their gardens to be photographed:

Chenies Manor, Buckinghamshire, Mrs Macleod-Matthews
Clinton Lodge, Sussex, Mr & Mrs Collum
Gopsall Pottery, Winchelsea, Sussex, Mike Crosby Jones
Hollington Nurseries, Berkshire, Simon & Judith Hopkinson
Old Place Farm, Kent, Mr & Mrs Jeffrey Eker
Rofford Manor, Oxfordshire, Mr & Mrs Mogford
Terence Conran's Chef Garden, RHS Flower Show, Chelsea
Warren Farm Cottages, Hampshire, Dr & Mrs Mitchell
West Dean Gardens, Sussex, Edward James Foundation
Whole Earth Foods, Portobello Road, London

Jonathan Buckley would particularly like to thank Judith and Simon Hopkinson at Hollington Nurseries and Sarah Wain at West Dean for their help throughout this project.

index

acknowledgements

The author would like to thank all those involved in bringing this book
to fruition: Anne Ryland, whose idea it was and who commissioned me to
write it; Marek Walisiewicz for his editing and suggestions; Paul Reid for his
design that brings the whole thing to life; and the illustrator, Richard Bonson,
who has gone to great pains to turn rough sketches into images; and last, but
not least, Jonathan Buckley, whose brilliant photographs make the book.

Thanks also go to all the owners who allowed Jonathan to photograph
their wonderful vegetable gardens for this book.